Bonjour Mr Inshaw

David Inshaw was born in Wednesfield, Staffordshire, in 1943 and grew up in Biggin Hill, Kent. He studied painting at Beckenham School of Art and the Royal Academy Schools. Between 1966 and 1975 he taught painting and printmaking at West of England College of Art, Bristol. Inshaw held a Fellowship in Creative Art at Trinity College, Cambridge, from 1975 to 1977, and was a member of the Brotherhood of Ruralists from 1975 to 1983. His work has appeared in many group and solo exhibitions and has been the subject of three BBC documentaries. He received an honorary doctorate of letters from the University of Durham in 2012.

Peter Robinson was born in Salford, Lancashire, in 1953 and grew up mainly in Liverpool. He holds degrees from the Universities of York and Cambridge. After teaching for many years in Japan, he returned to Europe in 2007 and is currently Professor of English and American Literature at the University of Reading. The poetry editor for Two Rivers Press, author of many books of poetry, translations, prose fiction, and literary criticism, he has been awarded the Cheltenham Prize, the John Florio Prize, and two Poetry Book Society Recommendations.

By the same author

Poetry

The Benefit Forms
Overdrawn Account
This Other Life
More about the Weather
Entertaining Fates
Lost and Found
About Time Too
Selected Poems 1976–2001
Ghost Characters
The Look of Goodbye
The Returning Sky
Buried Music
Collected Poems 1976–2016
Ravishing Europa

Prose & Interviews

Untitled Deeds
Talk about Poetry: Conversations on the Art
Spirits of the Stair: Selected Aphorisms
Foreigners, Drunks and Babies: Eleven Stories
The Draft Will
September in the Rain
The Constitutionals

Translations

The Great Friend and Other Translated Poems
Selected Poetry and Prose of Vittorio Sereni
The Greener Meadow: Selected Poems of Luciano Erba
Poems by Antonia Pozzi

Criticism

In the Circumstances: About Poems and Poets
Poetry, Poets, Readers: Making Things Happen
Twentieth Century Poetry: Selves and Situations
Poetry & Translation: The Art of the Impossible
The Sound Sense of Poetry

Also published by Two Rivers Press

The Art of Peter Hay by John Froy
English Martyrs by Conor Carvillle
Reaction Time of Glass by James Peake
Point of Honour by Maria Teresa Horta, translated
   by Lesley Saunders
Botanical Artistry by Julia Trickey
Penumbra by Kate Behrens
Pennies on my Eyes by Wilfred Owen
Precarious Lives by Jean Watkins
The Greenwood Trees by Christina Hart-Davies
Reading Abbey and the Abbey Quarter by Peter Durrant
   and John Painter
Reading's Bayeux Tapestry by Reading Museum
Sandpaper & Seahorses by John Froy
On Magnetism by Steven Matthews
Octopus Medicine by Becci Louise
Storms under the Skin by Henri Michaux, translated by
   Jane Draycott
Stanley Spencer Poems edited by Jane Draycott,
   Carolyn Leder & Peter Robinson
Half the Human Race by Susan Utting

Bonjour Mr Inshaw

Poems by Peter Robinson

Paintings by David Inshaw

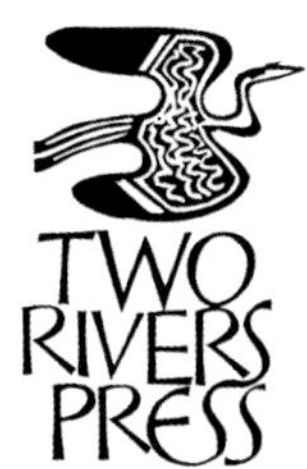

First published in the UK in 2020 by Two Rivers Press
7 Denmark Road, Reading RG1 5PA
www.tworiverspress.com

ISBN 978-1-909747-56-2

1 2 3 4 5 6 7 8 9

Two Rivers Press is represented in the UK by Inpress Ltd and distributed by NBNi.

Cover design by Nadja Guggi using David Inshaw's *Bonjour Mr Stockham* (1975), oil on canvas, 152×183cm
Text design by Nadja Guggi and typeset in Parisine and Janson

Printed and bound in Great Britain by Gomer Press, Ceredigion

Acknowledgements

'A Woman a Poem a Picture' also appeared in *Overdrawn Account* (London: The Many Press, 1980), *The Draft Will* (Tokyo and London: Isobar Press, 2015), and *Trinity Poets* ed. Adrian Poole and Angela Leighton (Manchester: Carcanet Press, 2017). 'After Inspiration' was prompted by a car journey with Jenny Lewis, the poem's dedicatee, taken on 9 January 2019. 'Swan' and 'Raptors', two of the parts from 'Postcard Concertina', appeared in *Noon: Journal of the Short Poem 14* (2019) and 'Slader's Yard' was published in *Shearsman 119 & 120* (2019).

Publisher's acknowledgements

The Publisher is extremely grateful to David Inshaw for granting permission to reproduce his wonderful artwork in this book, to Tabretts Fine Art Ltd for permission to use the digital files of David's work and to Libanus Press Ltd for making them available to us. We are also very grateful to the owners of the paintings that are reproduced here, many of whom we have been in touch with but there are some that we can't trace. We would be grateful for any information that would help us contact remaining owners who might like to know about this lovely book.

Contents

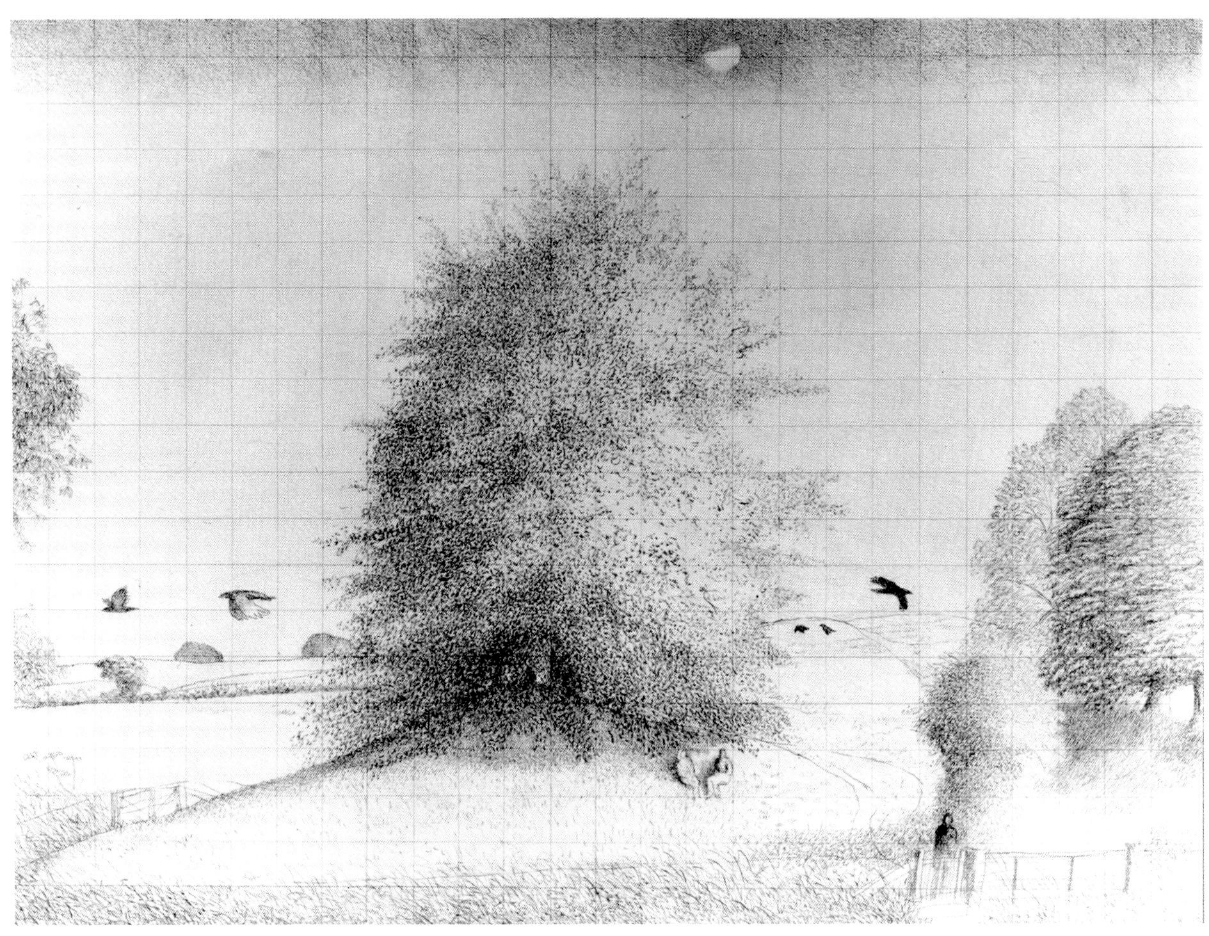

Study for Bonjour Mr Stockham (1974)
Pencil on paper, 52×66cm

Preface

David Inshaw and I were both attached, as chance would have it, to Trinity College, Cambridge, at the same time. I had gone up to work for a PhD, initially on Ezra Pound and the Visual Arts, in October 1975, the very same moment that David began his two-year stint as Fellow Commoner in Creative Arts. Sadly, though, we didn't meet until the following year at the earliest, while memory dates my fairly regular frequenting of his rooms to 1977, when my girlfriend and I were living behind the University Library in Herschel Road. As I imagine in one of the poems that follows, someone, perhaps it was Adrian Poole, a fellow of the college, must have told me of his existence – probably after I had been talking about my continuing desire, alongside other ambitions, to paint and draw.

During his time as Fellow Commoner, David was living in a suite of rooms on the first floor of the first staircase to the right in Neville's Court. As the poem 'In the Seventies' pieces it together, I must have climbed the stairs to the white-painted panel door on that first-floor landing, and been invited into rooms converted into a painter's studio. It was fairly crowded with works, including large drawings, and, if I remember rightly, *Presentiment* receiving some further touches. *The Letter* was resting there, and *Lovers Near Kew Gardens*, with its strange marks in the sky, marks explained by the picture's evolving on a piece of board used as a palette for colour mixing. Elgar's *The Dream of Gerontius* might well have been playing, and I was sat down on a sofa by the fireplace, offered tea – with honey, if I preferred – and given the advice, remembered ever since, not to stir the pot if you wanted a gentler brew, but to swivel it round a few times.

Glimpses from a few other visits to those rooms come back, including his mentioning an early poem of mine called 'Overdrawn Account', which was published in that year's *Trinity Review*. Next to it – not my work or choice – was a horridly mannered black-and-white ink drawing of a clown, which had so offended David's visual taste and imagination that he had covered it over in his copy. As noted in 'After Courbet', he was working on *The Orchard*, and talked about his difficulties with it – not that you'd think there had been any from how it came out in the end.

Our acquaintance continued more sporadically after he left Cambridge, where I remained for another three years attempting to complete the PhD, which had by then evolved into a study of contemporary poetry called *Responsibilities and Distances*, a painterly sort of moralizing title. My then wife Rosie and I visited him at his house in Lansdowne Terrace, Devizes, after a rather washed-out camping holiday in the Cotswolds in September 1978. We coincided at the private view of his retrospective exhibition in Brighton in the autumn of that same year, and were invited to dinner with David and Robin – and served pigeon – during the time when they were living together in Cambridge, probably a year later. My first collection, *Overdrawn Account*, came out from the Many Press in November 1980. It contained the prose poem dedicated to David called 'A Woman a Poem a Picture'. This had been composed in 1977 and handwritten onto my pencil drawing of a young woman walking with her head bowed, given to the painter in gratitude for his advice and friendship before he left Cambridge. An inscribed copy of the book with a letter enclosed was posted to him when it appeared.

The following February, though, I began my own Welsh interlude when offered a two-year temporary lectureship at Aberystwyth. I was still, of course, aware of David's work, not least when teaching Shakespeare from the new Arden editions with covers by the Brotherhood of Ruralists. There followed a period of over thirty years in which our only further meeting took place entirely by chance in the lobby of the Royal Academy. I'm not able exactly to date this coincidental encounter, but think it might have been in the 1990s. It was certainly after his marriage to Robin had ended, because I asked after her, and possibly after his own Welsh phase, and it may have been around the time of the Waddington exhibition in 1998, because I still have an invitation to that show.

It had been very nice to see him, and he had been as friendly as ever, but it didn't seem possible or realistic to keep up our acquaintance, however much I might have liked to do so. Nevertheless, almost another decade after my repatriation in 2007, Adrian contacted me about an anthology that was being assembled, bringing together many of the poets associated, one way or another, with Trinity College, Cambridge. Here was an occasion to allow 'A Woman a Poem a Picture' to have another airing, and, in my note looking back to those early years as a graduate student, I naturally mentioned how much of a pleasure and inspiration it had been to meet David Inshaw.

The launch of the *Trinity Poets* anthology in September 2017 was organized to coincide with a reunion for the Fellow Commoners in Creative Arts – and this is how I found myself, after all those years, seated for the dinner next to David and his partner Louise. Though catching up, we talked as if no time had passed at all. There followed meetings at the Slader's Yard Gallery in the autumn of that year, and a visit to Devizes to see the studio with my wife Ornella the following spring, and then again in the autumn at West Bay once more, since we happened to be spending the weekend in Lulworth Cove. Further conversations flowed and I added a couple of poems set on the Dorset coast, and included here, to my old prose poem from 1977.

The final element in the occasions for the sequence of poems that follows came about through some further coincidences. I was visiting the house of the Oxford poet Jenny Lewis, and happened to notice a book about the painter Margaret Mellis written by Andrew Lambirth. Jenny mentioned that he had also written a book about her friend David Inshaw. She then brought out her pencil drawing by David, showing the artist in a dreamt flight, and was telling me about plans she had put aside many years before to write a form of poetic biography of the painter. Out of this conversation came the idea that we might go down to Devizes together and discuss the project. Though I accompanied Jenny on that journey on 9 January 2019 in the role of potential publisher, while we were together, David suggested I might write some poems too. Doubtless thanks in part to the crisis we were all living through, and with an alacrity that more than surprised me, drafting the majority of the sequence in a little over three weeks, that's exactly what I proceeded to do.

Peter Robinson
July 2019

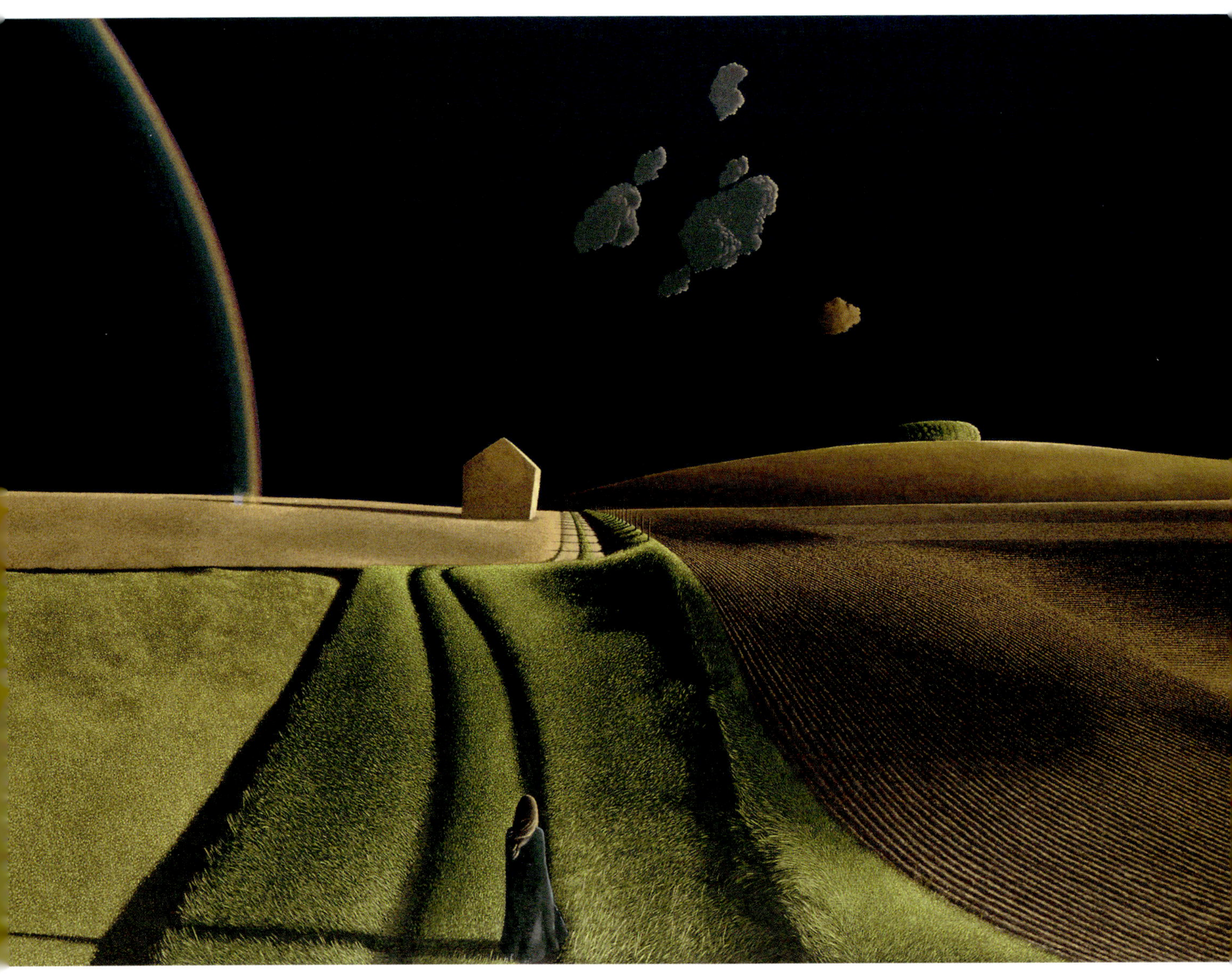

A Woman a Poem a Picture

for David Inshaw

The flattened cumulus darker than slate allows bright sunshine to break across the gap between cloud banks and the tumuli as, elsewhere, topiary hedges.

Would it be a woman reaches up to readjust her – what's it called? – a parasol. Or, no, she waves goodbye.

Dilapidated circumstances: lacking its flimsy white covering, Thomas Hardy ('greatest of the moderns') imagined the one he had come across a skeleton. Well, he would.

The deepening presence of … what if she leaves him? Clouds are heaped. A mackerel sky has evening written all over it. Not very much gets finished. Now you count two women, together, playing shuttlecock. Best to keep it under your hat was William Blake's advice, for love that's told can never be.

And she has turned face into the sun. The yellow verso of her breasts diminishing, this shadow may well be extended – and to whatsoever distance. Embed small dabs of darker tone in the field behind her.

It's difficult to draw with the woman in his light. The painter has set up his easel in that green, but his model refuses, point-blank, to stand still.

At the Invitation View, it remains unclear who has returned and from what oblique, unwished-for angle. The colour match depends on whatever she is wearing: no, hardly the original air-blue gown. It's the unexpected appearance of another person's wife, who stops herself from smiling, and goes on up the stairs.

She Did Not Turn (1974)
Oil on canvas, 137×183cm

1977

After Inspiration

for Jenny Lewis

Uninterrupted, mid-winter sunlight
comes clear and bright after days of grey,
the transitory blossom
real as you like on reminiscent boughs
when even this January weather
looks more than inclined to collaborate
with a journey undertaken
down to Devizes, and desired inspiration.

The short day's brightness promises
more substance later on
in the form of jockeys' coloration
beside white rails, their training paddock,
the horses lined up in a row,
they too collaborating
at a gambol or a gamble, oh,
as if to test the limits of our luck!

Then keeping off the motorway
we'll take a route you'd likely take
through this chilly season
now and in England, as well I might say
(you see I've put the war in too);
we're skirting hedgerows, copses, signs,
whilst talking out conflicted
disasters of the métier.

Despondency, madness, envy or the spite,
how they'll blast you, blighting, after inspiration!

2019

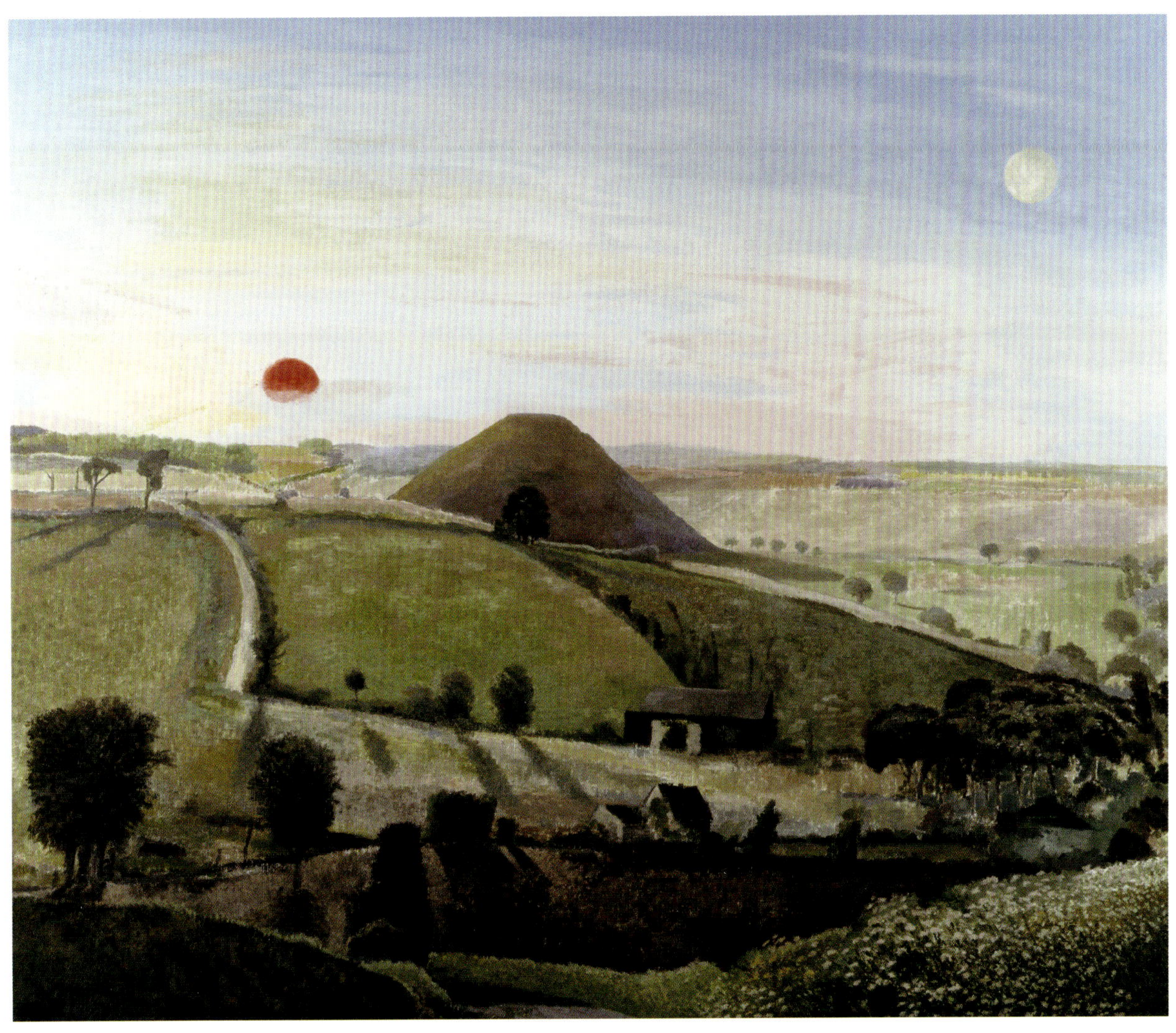

Wiltshire Landscape, Silbury Hill in the Distance (1985)
Oil on canvas, 130×145cm

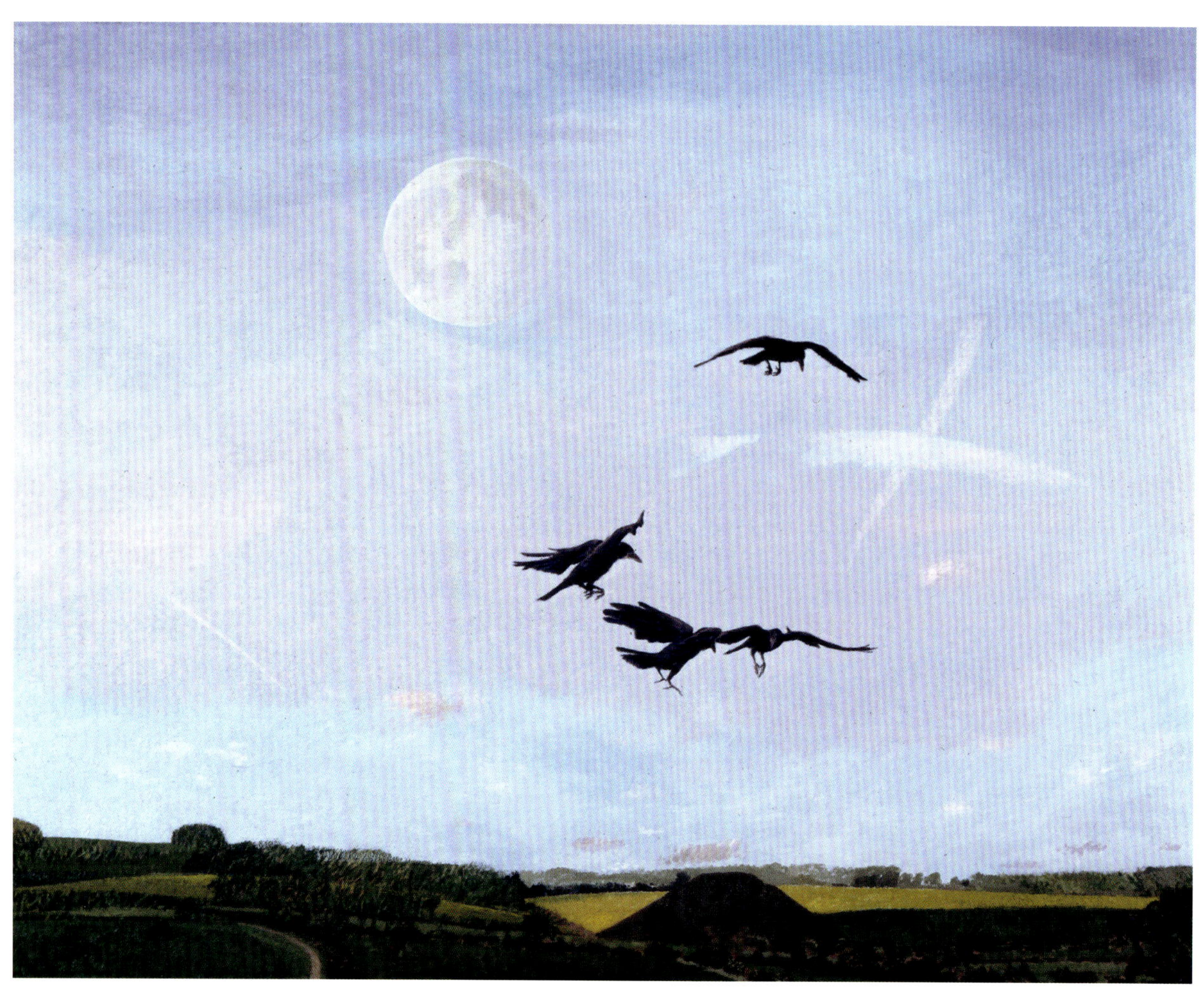

Wiltshire Landscape (1987–88)
Oil on canvas, 130×152cm

Bonjour Mr Inshaw

You see the day would be propitious
descending now by Silbury Hill
this antithesis of summer;
we would follow road-sign arrows
pointing at a daylight moon
with, maybe, overflying crows,
fallow fields, a ploughed one,
views, the recognizable
Wiltshire landscape opening
to anthologies of cloud.

These chilly, deepened shadows,
shadows cast by rival wills are
stretched by sun low in the sky;
but laid to rest between us
this bitterly divided season
when history is England now,
now and again, each shadow
stirs a moment as we pass
Alf Stockham, Hardy, someone
leant upon a coppice gate.

Beyond those tree-clump ridges,
three realist figures, imagine,
are rendered on a fictive scene;
also, in the here-and-now,
a freely sketched parked car …
For if you want to understand
it's best to go at least half way
and meet our painter on his ground
with a 'Bonjour, Monsieur Inshaw'
at the moss-green front door.

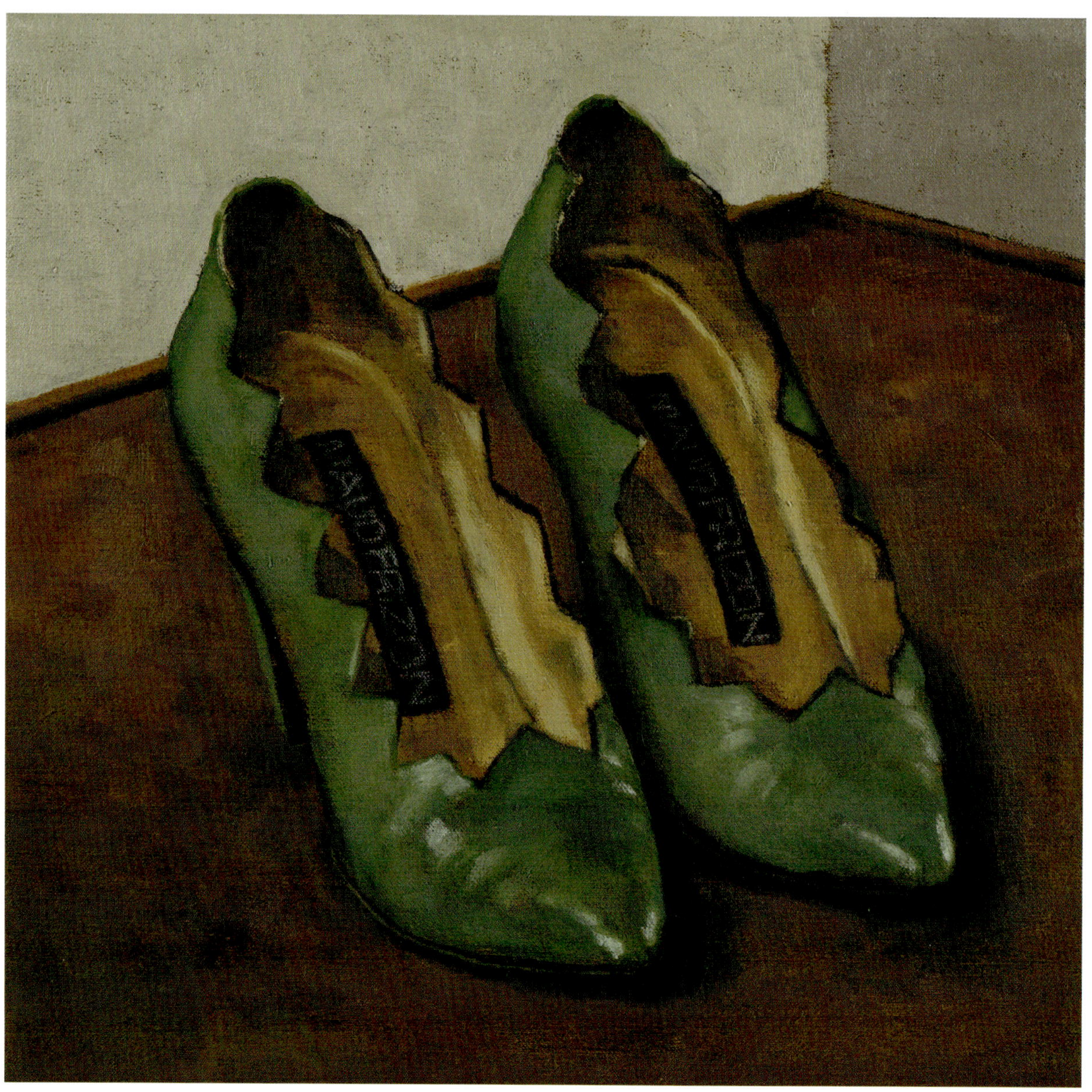

Some Recollections

'... an orderly hoarder.'
Andrew Lambirth

Kept tidily, your collaged feelings
on stretched Belgian canvases,
the new or reworked, stacked
like people you have lost, old mentors,
missed Christmas cards, and fear to find
at our age how they might have died,
are pointed to in words and things.
It brings them back, time out of mind,
as bodies sense themselves at home
getting reacquainted.

From further still, your memories
going and the mislaid names
and how we might have come to meet
are startled by a pair
of shark-tooth-shaped green shoes, Miss Julie's,
these still-life objects remaining behind
after they've been painted.

Cheryl's Shoes (2012)
Oil on canvas, 12×12 inches

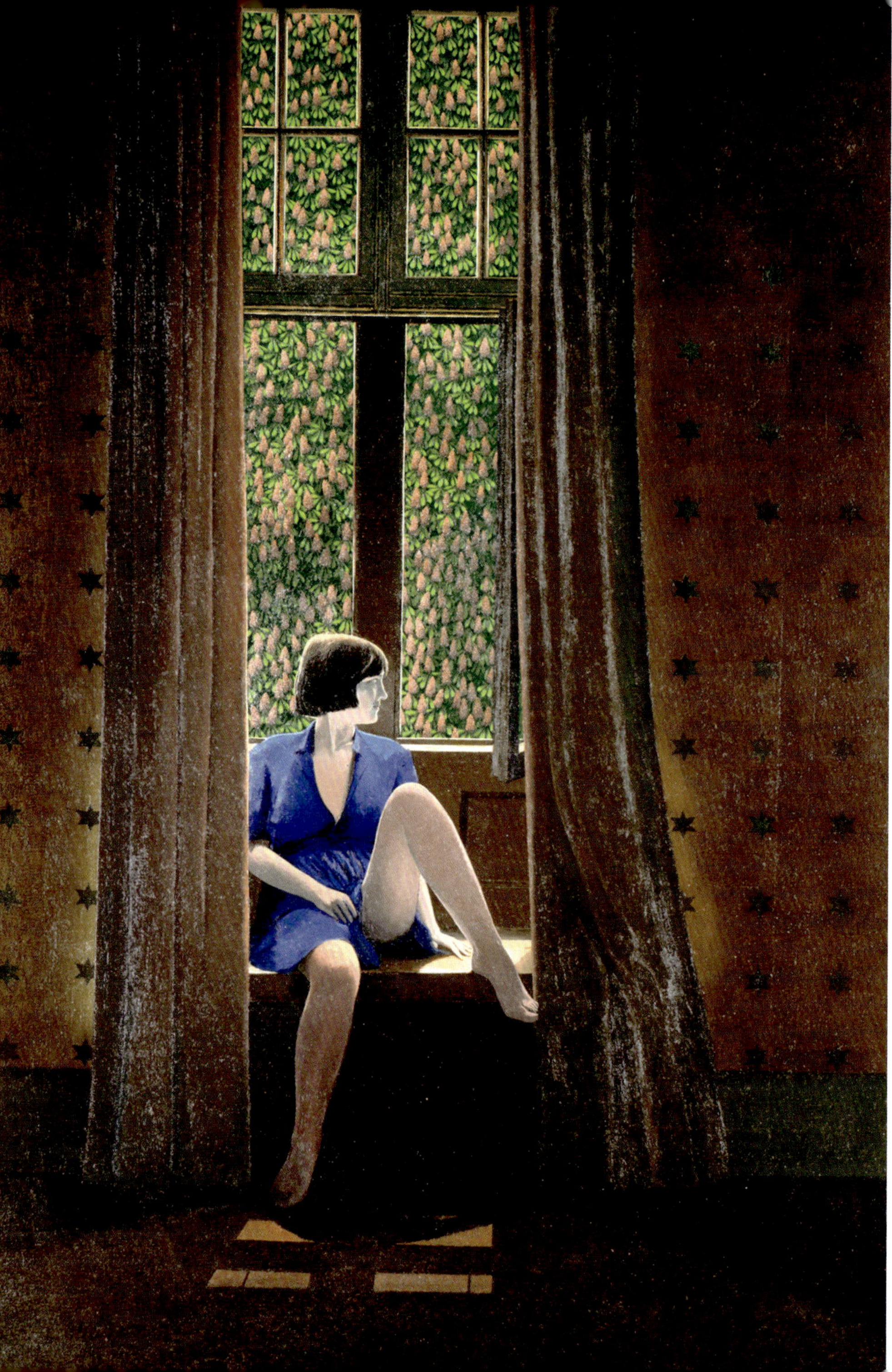

In the Seventies

'Locked in me.'
Thomas Hardy

But how it was we came to meet
more than forty years ago,
that too would have to be invented
from patched hints, fragmented
snatches of an atmosphere
or prompts such as the Balthus
girl poised on a window seat,
one knee raised in the curtained gloom
while up behind her head
proportioned panes replete
with sunlit chestnut candles
bring May to the Old Guest Room.

Someone must have mentioned you.
Then I'll have climbed that creaky stair,
been offered tea and conversation,
later, given good advice –
how best to make a flesh-tone
without black in its shadow …
while leant against your mantelpiece
was that one on a palette board,
sketchily imagined, the *Lovers near Kew*,
their kissing heads, an English flag
with meaning, hapless, altered now,
and her dress of a polka-dot blue.

Veronica, Old Guest Room,
Trinity College, Cambridge (1976–78)
Oil on canvas, 127×79cm

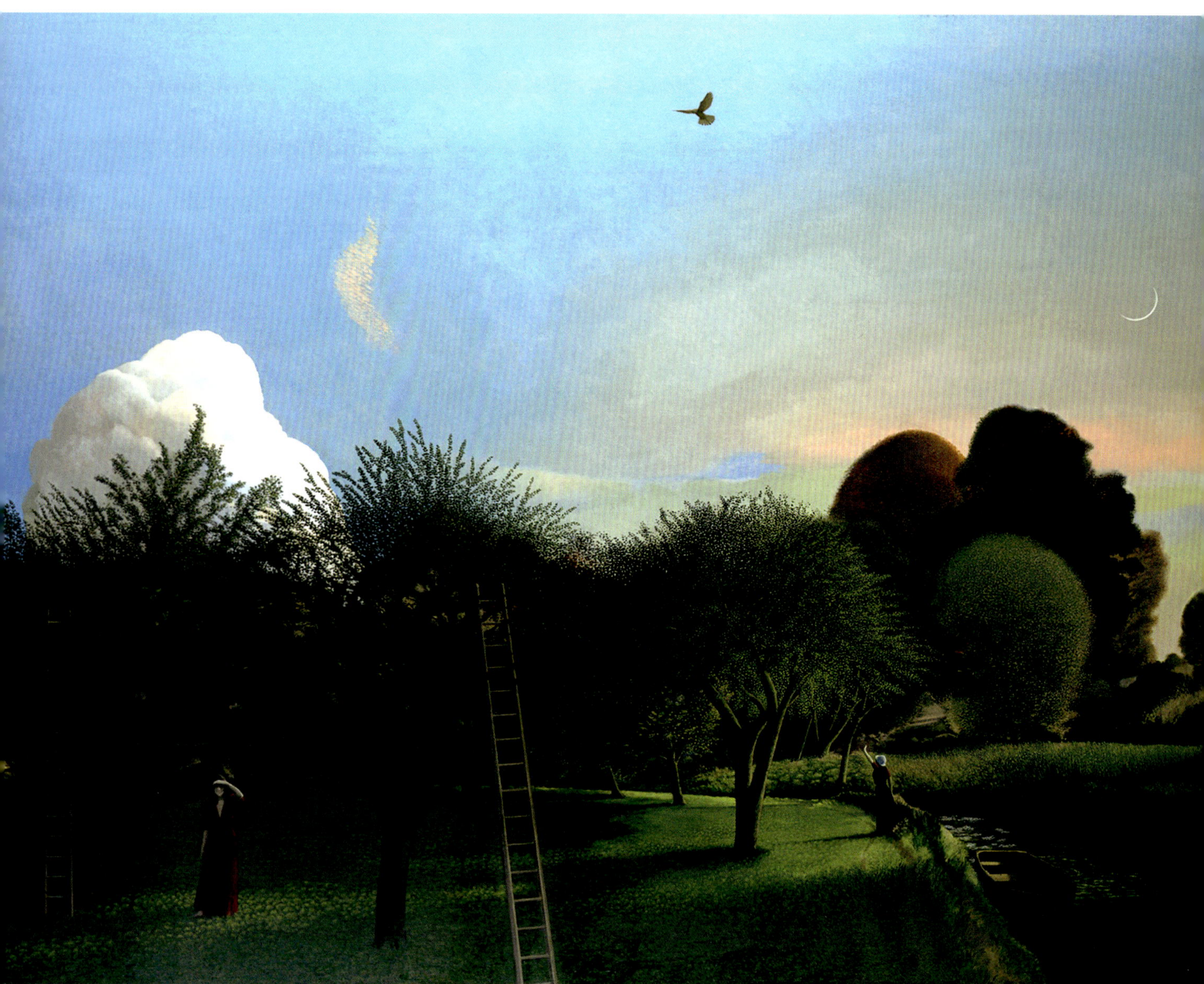

After Courbet

You were working on *The Orchard*.
We talked about its foreground ladder,
the feet secured, it seemed, nowhere
on that unresponsive canvas
with tension problem, sunken paint
where one girl's reaching, as for apples,
the other stares, oh distant women –
and two more in *The Letter*, naked,
precise pudenda like a wound
relating troubles of my own
as Courbet's *L'Origine du monde*
in women even I had known.

The Orchard (1977)
Oil on canvas, 122×183cm

Haunting Landscapes

Haunted, pursued by your earlier work,
see, they return, those ones
like *The Badminton Game*, or a dark-haired
woman glancing round between headstones
in a graveyard where 'our days
were a joy and our paths through flowers';
topiary, storm clouds, seated girl with raven
come back like the one who didn't turn
from that other Hardy poem …

Each blade of grass, brick course and ripple,
whether through water, leafage or sky
dryly individuated stills its still point
into a distanced reminiscence –
whatever sticks to things like burrs
evacuated now …

But time you stop won't go away.
Perpetually present, it has to stay
replete with others' meanings
from gallery walls, gone into the world
of chiaroscuro, image, reputation,
not knowing how or why.

Yet, still, there are the earlier ones
like *Paris* via *Victoria Dover Calais*,
your feelings for a fish, girl, plane
or mine about a poem, a picture
that keep their wistful promises –
blued clouds above sunset horizons
traipsing through our day.

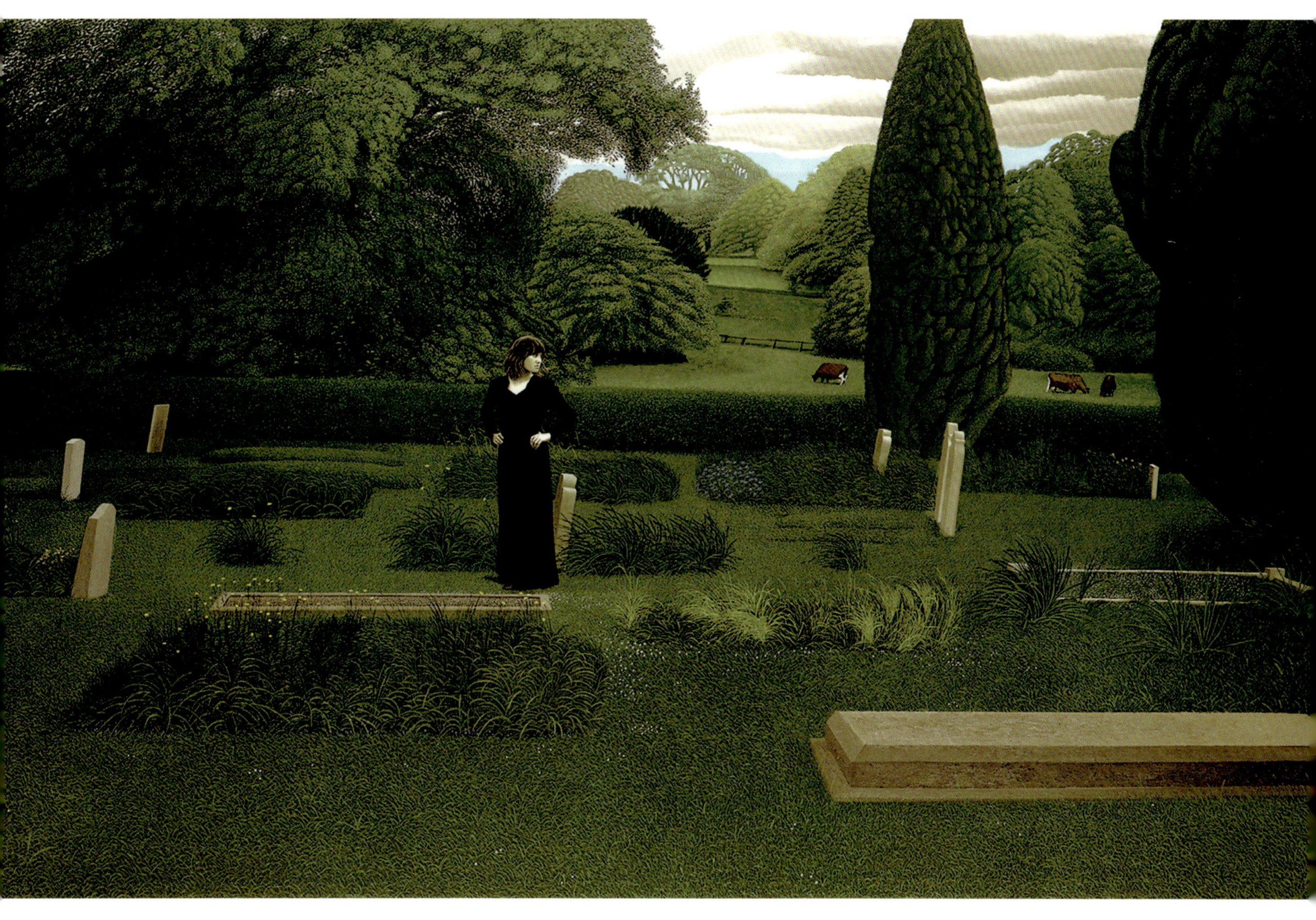

Our days were a joy and our paths through flowers (1972)
Oil on canvas, 137×213 cm

Mr Manners

Background music touching my ear
might be '*tristezza, per favore va via*'
as far from treasons, stratagems and spoils
we're here in a basement bit of Italy –
its red-checked table cloths and murals'
vistas like a *bella* Naples …

Then a morsel from one sea-bass dish
catches all of our attentions –
whether left to fend off shame
or a forfeit for virility,
as she'd explain, their front-of-house,
clearing up that finished plate.

Hesitant whether to stop or stay
I was holding open an inner door,
saw your painting arm move in its frame …
So even *il pezzo della vergogna*
must mean – I'd think – to collaborate
on the meaning of this scene.

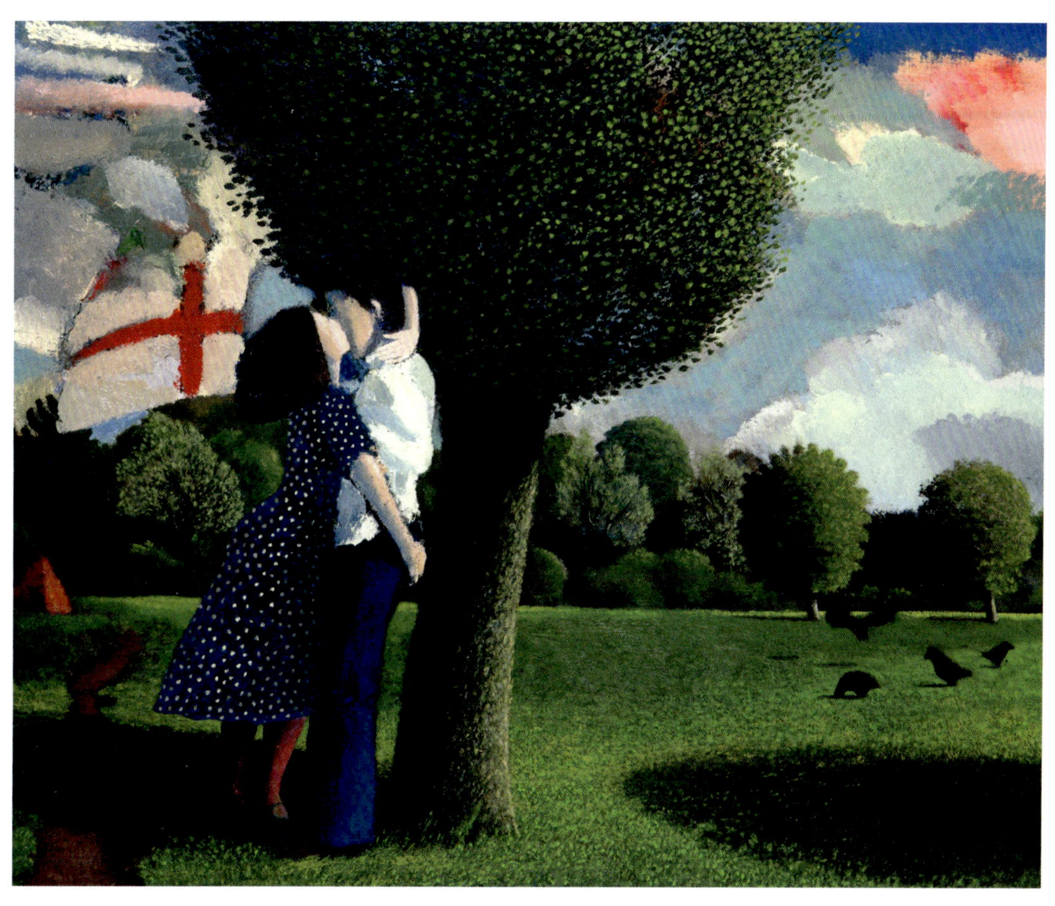

Lovers near Kew Gardens (1976)
Oil on board, 32×37cm

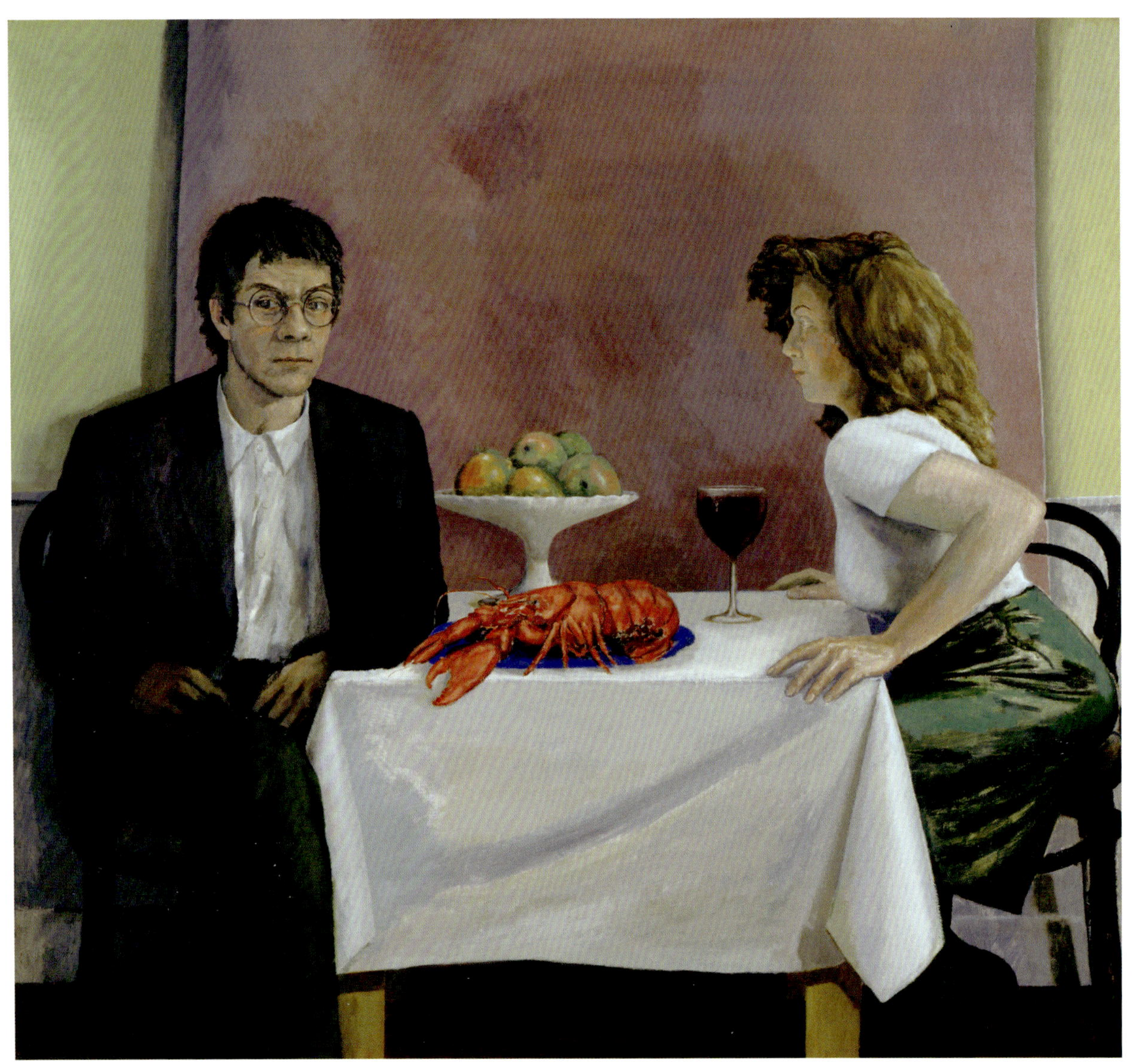

Conversation Piece

But whatever had they been talking about?
Tight-lipped, the grimly serious
self-portrait glancing out at us …

She's rising from their restaurant table,
like a Rembrandt syndic at Amsterdam!
Ambiguous, her wide-eyed stare
dismisses the lobster, red between them,
that glass of burgundy untouched
or our painter, the *haute cuisine* …
They're making a meal of things today.

His painted-out gesture à la Degas
and all the other *pentimenti*
(her blouse's loose white sleeves,
him bearded in the pencil study)
they're imaginably, visibly there
as though regrets at a might-have-been
(their food uneaten, tasteless, still)
would be the meaning of that scene.

The Meal (1989–95)
Oil on canvas, 122×130cm

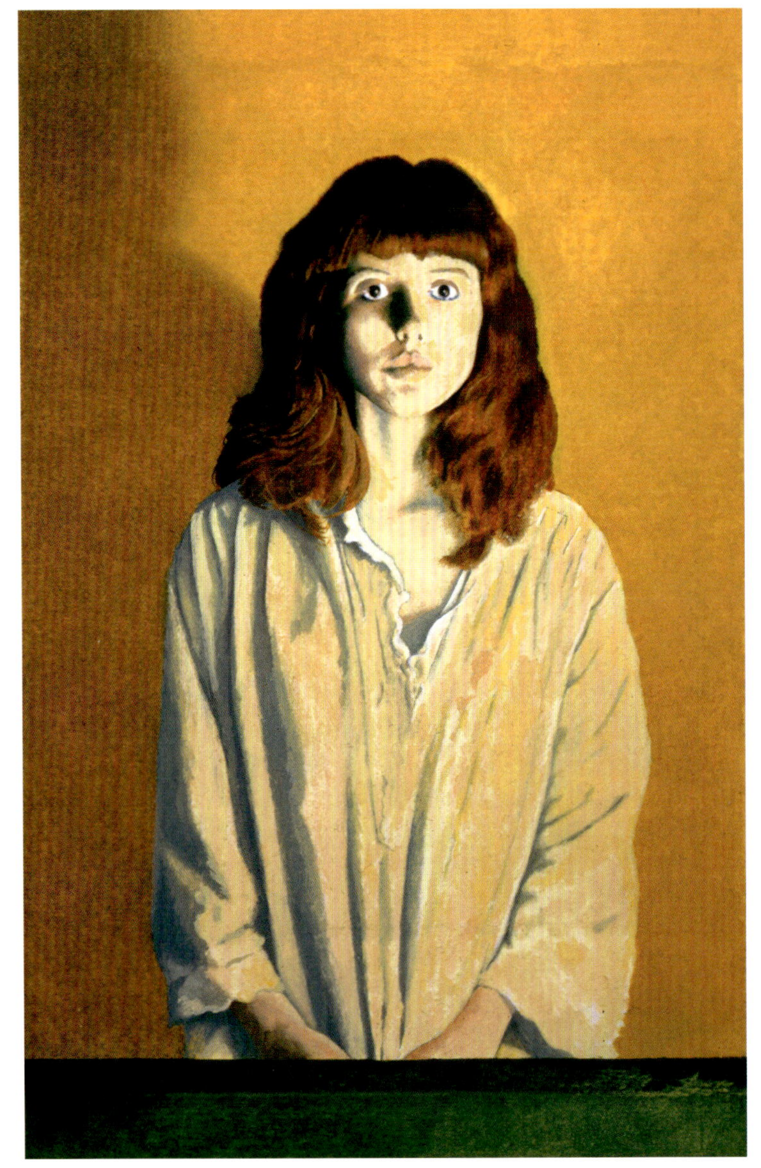

Back Door Moments

'I doubt it not, and all these woes shall serve
For sweet discourses in our times to come.'
William Shakespeare, *Romeo and Juliet*

We had stepped in and out of your studio:
a converted chapel where each mentor,
memento and material would, I know,
furnish the visual language meant for

leavening its centuries' devotional quiet;
here, still, now, feeling slowly forms
as Alfred Wallis depicting a yacht
might brush in the bow-wave's foams.

Black and white, half-timbered, silent,
'a piece of Shakespeare out the back!'
Shown how you usually came and went,

I suddenly said those very words, struck
as if by remembrance of things they meant:
time out of mind, oh Juliet, what luck …

Juliet (1980)
Oil on board, 23×15cm

The Galleries

'We can't allow photography in this exhibition
for copyright reasons. There's no copyright on
this wonderful view so you may photograph it
from here using a handheld camera, no flash.'
At *Jackson Pollock: Blind Spots* (2015)

1. TATE LIVERPOOL

Although I'm gazing out the window,
this is not a photograph
nor copyrighted picture, either.

Look here you see me throwing lines
out towards the image edge
'like thoughts, mad maps of all our days'
and though the restless, lapping waters
abut on dock-gates, customs house,
a gunboat (dazzle camouflaged),
they're projected from one point of view;

it flies out like a Peter Pan
to nothing but the world, composed
at random by this captioned frame
and instituted silences –
a red lightship, an ice cream van …

2. THE FRICK

Warned away from another window
and told to remain on the rug by a guard,
I can't but think that curtained view
of Central Park and Avenue,
it must have at least as much value
as e.g. Rembrandt's *Polish Rider* …

and though not thinking to steal a glimpse
of skeletal trees, mute traffic,
that window onto Central Park,
it's not what we paid our admission-fee for
(which is why, like a coat or a hat,
you could only check it out at the door).

3. MOMA

Signs of a restaurant or a corner bar,
some place in the Fifties,
now I glimpse them like a low relief
through one more gallery window
amongst big gestures, scrawls, designs,
the pop on a transistor radio
played from out its lost decade
and to me that nondescript shadowy street,
it might have signaled back as art!

In the High Street

1.

Gone out the front to re-park Jenny's car,
not art, more like its opposite
we'd found in hurried spaces
and clutter from another disintegrating day –
shop signs, knock-down prices, faces,
the marketplace's facing stone
held up by plate glass, window dressing!

2.

One moment, stepped from that grey car,
I was gazing off, distracted;
you put an arm about my shoulder,
commiserating, brotherly,
as like from conclusions of imagined pain
at meaning in street scenery,
unpainted, for the consolation …

3.

Then the pavement edge as we walked back
and time on an overhanging clock,
they point towards departure …
but seeing through others' eyes resolves
that confusion of particulars
become world-gazes where a future
looks to save things from themselves.

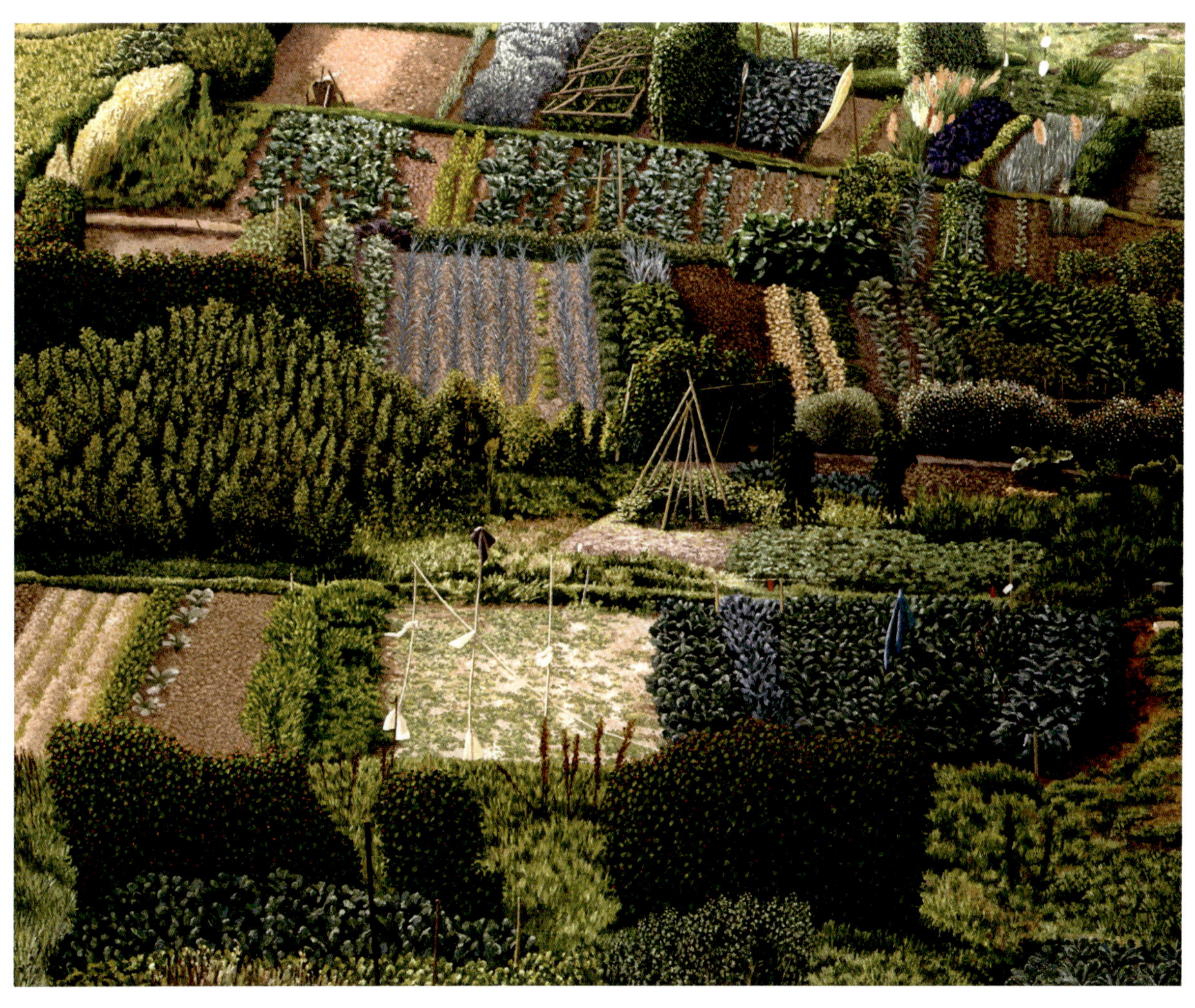

Allotments (1988)
Oil on canvas, 130×152cm

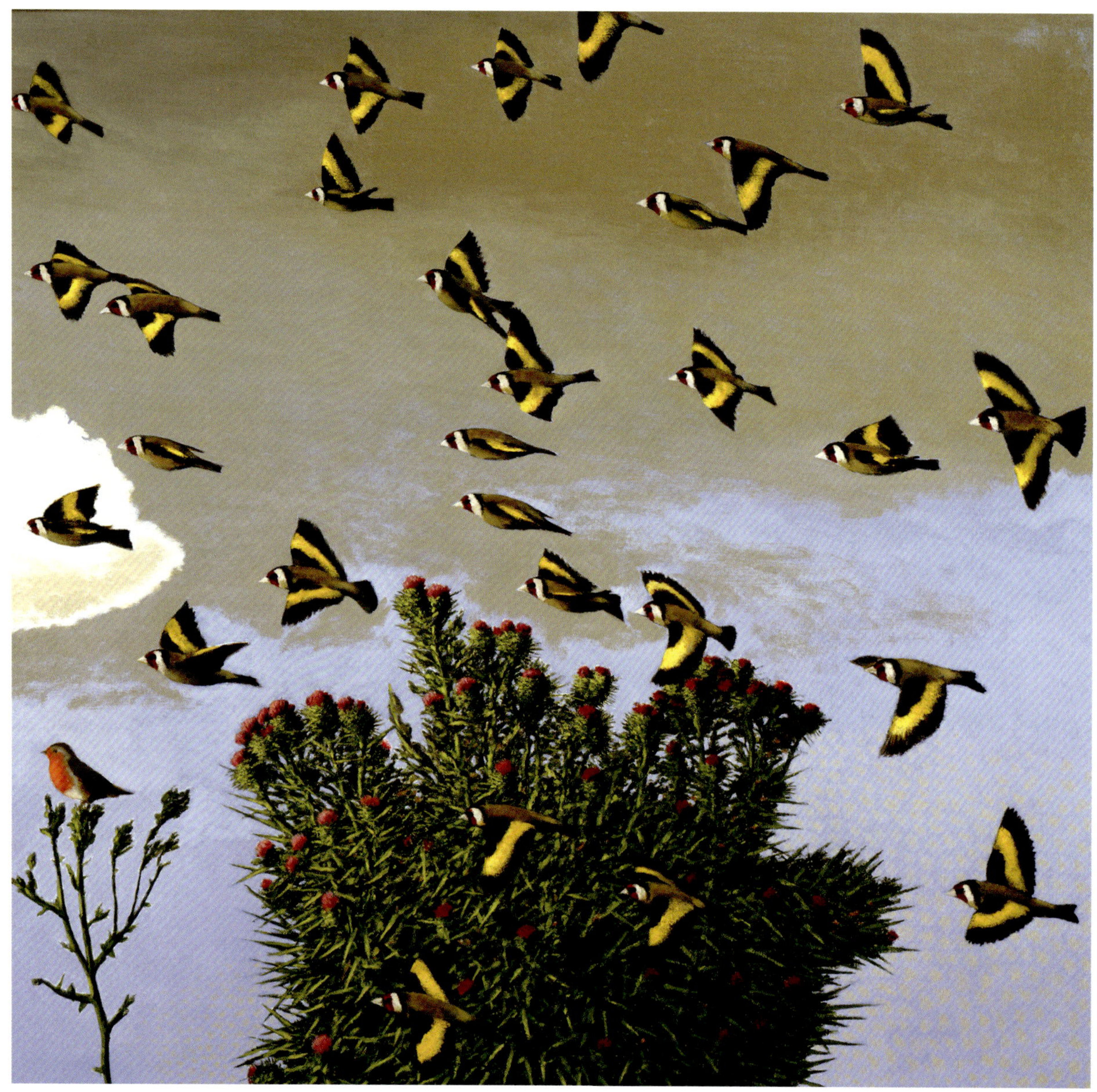

A Postcard Concertina

'This makes it possible to be ashamed of one's
country, and to feel a victim of moral bad luck'
Thomas Nagel, *Mortal Questions*

1. DEAD BIRDS

'Here there was a great mortality of birds'
across the chronicled countryside
with its bonfires, chalk erectile-giant
grown misted, sombre, distant,
a poor dead robin redbreast
and thistles, mistle thrushes …

But not chained up as in Fabritius,
still I see them rise on air,
around a single, perching robin,
those emblems, all the yellow-flashes,
your squadron of free finches!

2. PARLIAMENT

But when the noises off come back
lacking all conviction or
with passionate intensity,
we're baffled at the best of times –

as if by a parliament of fowls,
one starling still among pale catkins,
bullfinch, swallow, owls,
no end to their palaver …

Goldfinches (2003–4)
Oil on canvas, 91×91cm

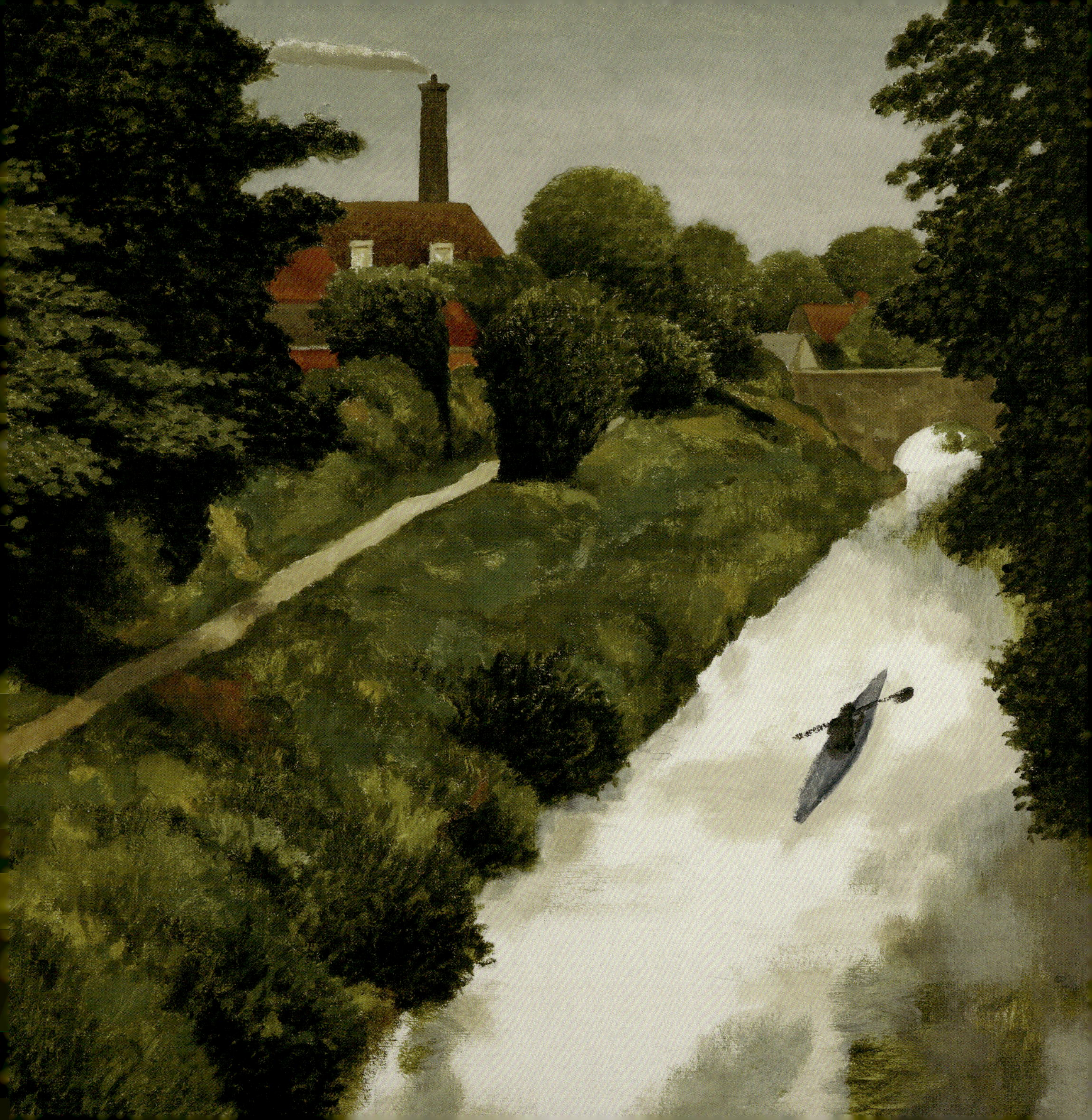

3. STILL POINT

Now when a full moon
up behind bare ruined boughs,
flint-shard walls of cloisters,

finds cold deepening
you've rushed to the station
winded, in first dawn,

and frosts, the sun's rays
dazzle while long shadows
point nowhere at all!

4. THE KENNET

That rising, super, blood, wolf moon
above our Huntley & Palmers'
red-brick, named façade
is reflected in a watery mirror
at this far end of the Kennet canal.

It's the same as at Devizes, painted
with feeling for your scenery
compromised by voices, pained
magical thinking, venery
and, mercy me, the strained
trust in being here, love tainted.

Canal at Devizes (2010)
Oil on canvas, 61×61 cm

5. SWAN

Now from a start-of-year
emptiness I hear
another inland seagull's cry –
like someone asking why
I should even care
now this or other outcome
has been put, rehashed, rehearsed,
oh, *ad infinitum*?

At which I had to wonder
how such-a-body could even ask
when care too seems an alibi,
a parochial concern;
and down the slow canal,
smoothly there, a swan
is riding its reflection?

6. SECRET PORTRAITS

Urged to 'come together as a nation',
betraying values they can't show
are emptied, what starts from this window
are nostalgias without object
for a home that isn't there –
which I'd lament as much as you
with your sycamore, beech, your oak trees
filling out another view.

Its fold or hangar, pasture, plough,
the shades of night extending,
find people, unnamed, in that landscape,
wives or lovers, friends on bridges …
and still they're recognizable,
our comforts in such times as these.

Swan (1999)
Oil on canvas, 51×51cm

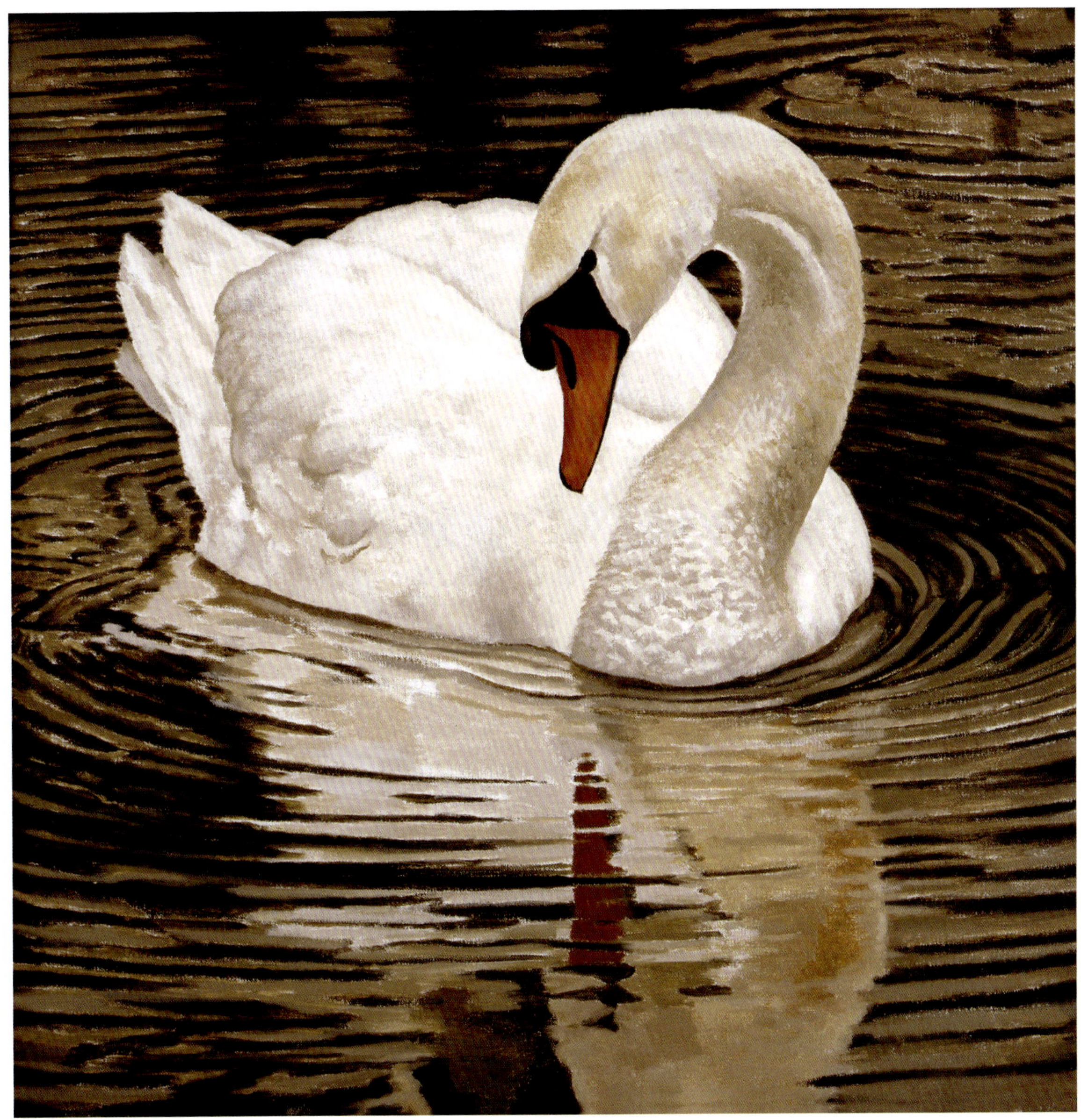

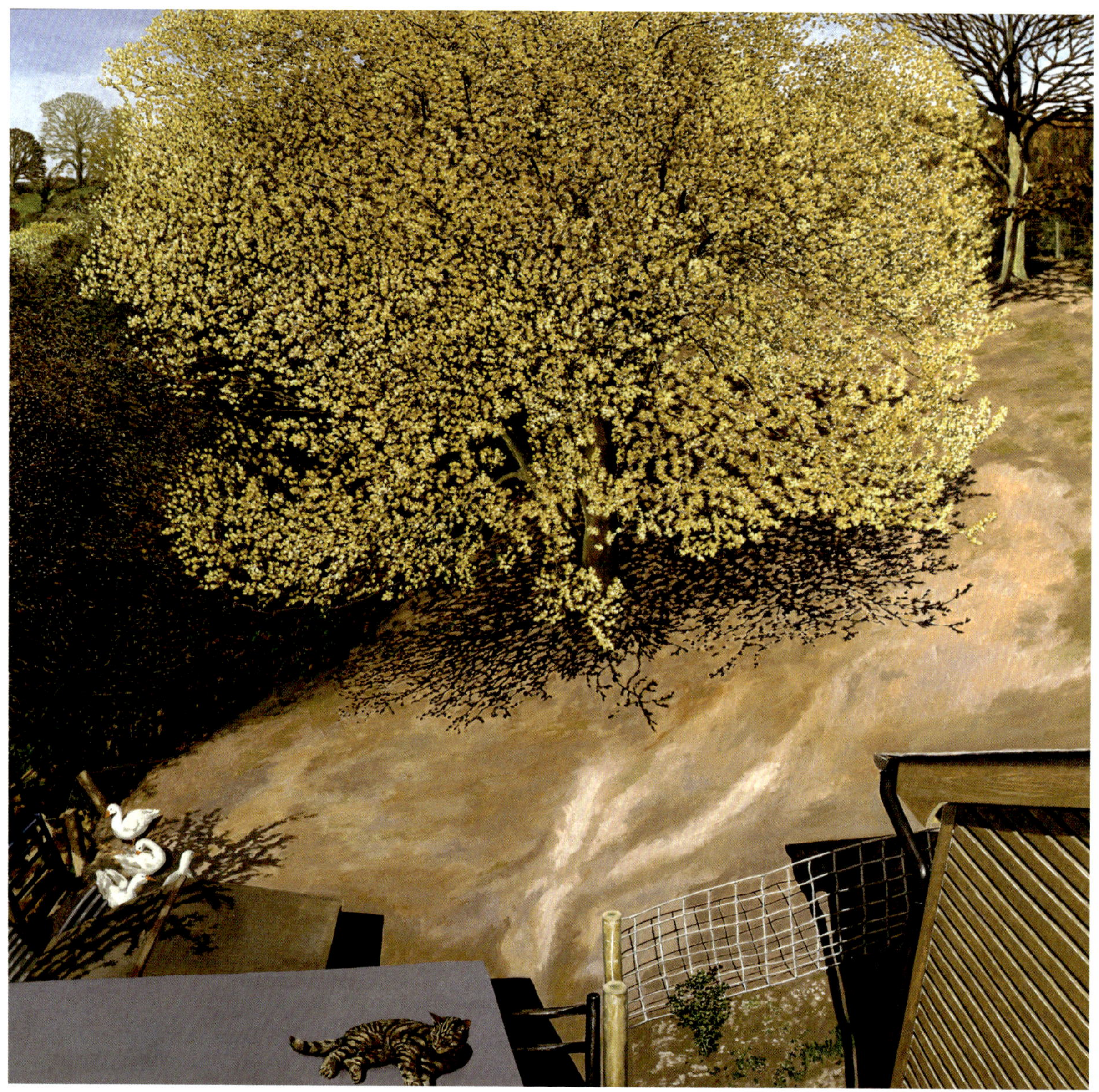

7. PUSSY WILLOW

Your leaping or your sleeping cat
beside that pussy willow tree
recall one lost down our back alley
in feral flowers and moonlight.

Anxious on a summer night,
restive, and trying to fall asleep,
I listened to its owner call,
'Come on now, boy, come on now!'

To tell the truth, she'd warned me
handing out her notices,
a photo of the stray pet on them;
but he's not coming home …

8. INCIDENTS

Your heart goes out to the rearing hare
swooped at by a tawny owl,
is stirred by hawks, kites, darker
wings upraised before attack,
and rises, flown above the ground
in someone else's aeroplane …

It's an invite not to disinvest
in country or the countryside,
but catch up on the left behind
of Cornwall, Wiltshire, Somerset,
anywhere now both sun and moon
are present with you in the sky.

Pussy Willow (1998–2004)
Oil on canvas, 152×152cm
(destroyed by fire 2015)

9. RAPTORS

Through those strains of suffering
a politician, pre-disgraced,
I'm remembering still the shame
we're born with, now their sure
ambitions for our country
flap like some white-paper dove;
and all of the above
is an interim report and love,
however unrequited, you're
the only deal I'm offering.

10. FULFILLMENT

Then from my lips slipped out *fulfillment*.
'Now there's a word,' is what you said
beside the signs of all it meant
uniting hand, eye, heart and head.

That's how the things we love can happen –
as back-turned women lean at windows
to keep their options open
in aid of some fulfillment, too, God knows.

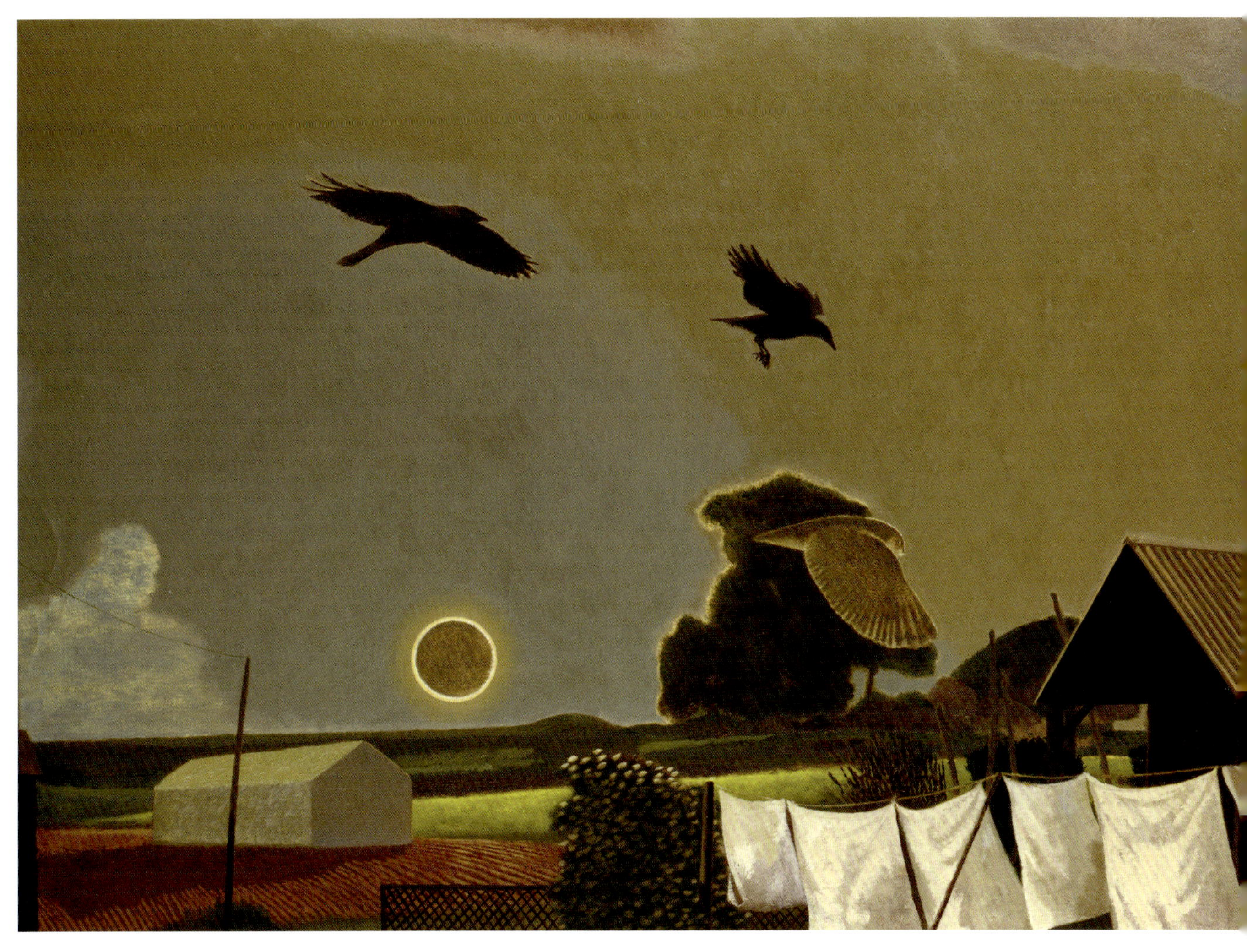

A Dramatic Incident in the Wiltshire Landscape (1984)
Oil on canvas, 58×81cm

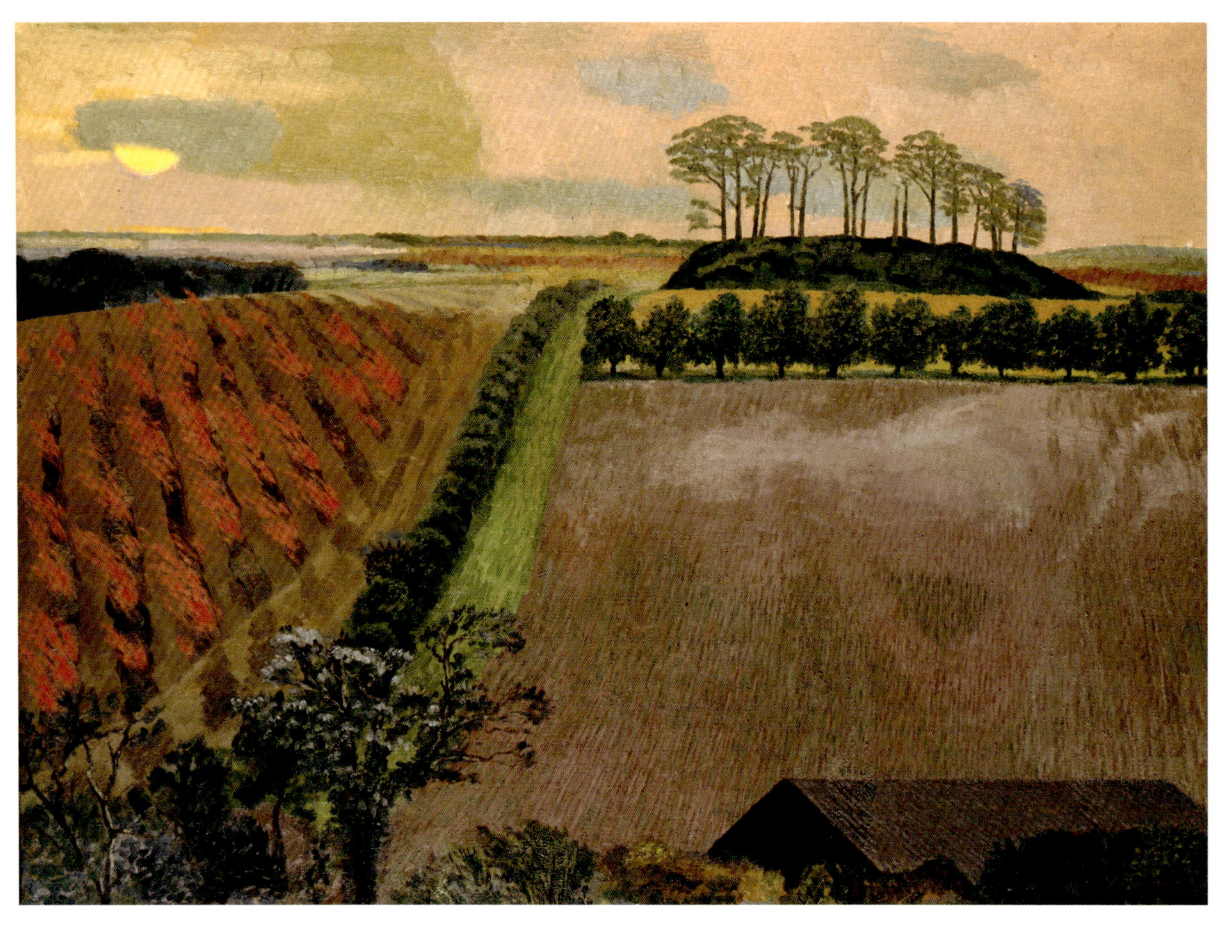

East Kennet Long Barrow (1985–87)
Oil on canvas, 76×102cm

Remembered Scenes

'and things begin to be
hopelessly strange to us'
Bernard Williams

Steam-wisps billow from outhouse chimneys
over frost-crisped fields' grisaille,
and a mackerel sky at daybreak
in fainter turquoise paints pink streaks;

then as on early trains –
look out, see feathery leafless trees'
mildewed trunks in scrubland
poke soft tufts above low skylines.

*

Last snow remnants down embankments
shrink further under mizzling rain,
and great bird congregations
come feeding together on hardened ground.

Not long beyond the shortest day
this landscape's eked-out sunlight's blighted;
rutted paths, a bridleway
are branching off to left and right …

*

As exiles belonging at a distance know
remembered scenes, the women
they've loved, that earthwork hump
at Maiden Castle or *East Kennet Long Barrow*,

sights of hedge, copse and a beech clump
redouble uprooted determinations
to feel at home somewhere –
as exiles belonging at a distance know!

*

But leaving behind this cloud-baulked sunrise,
what returns can't be the past
because where we are now land lies
closing down each possible

through stretches of allotments, small farms,
patchworks like a fractured parish
whose stubborn points and cumulus forms
they want to set at one.

*

But where a Hobbema's or Hodler's boughs
along your *West Wood* avenue
shape canopies filtered through with sun's rays,
still you come advancing views

of dark birds wheeling above that wish –
as nothing can be set at one
when words to atone or make amends
are truly, well, long gone –

*

and, look, like that *Storm over Silbury Hill*,
what returns can't be the past
for all of this is now,
now and yet again in England,

bare branches composed like an allegory's
assembled symbols to make it true,
if you see what I'm saying
in the light of your lightning-struck trees.

West Wood (2012)
Oil on canvas, 117×117cm

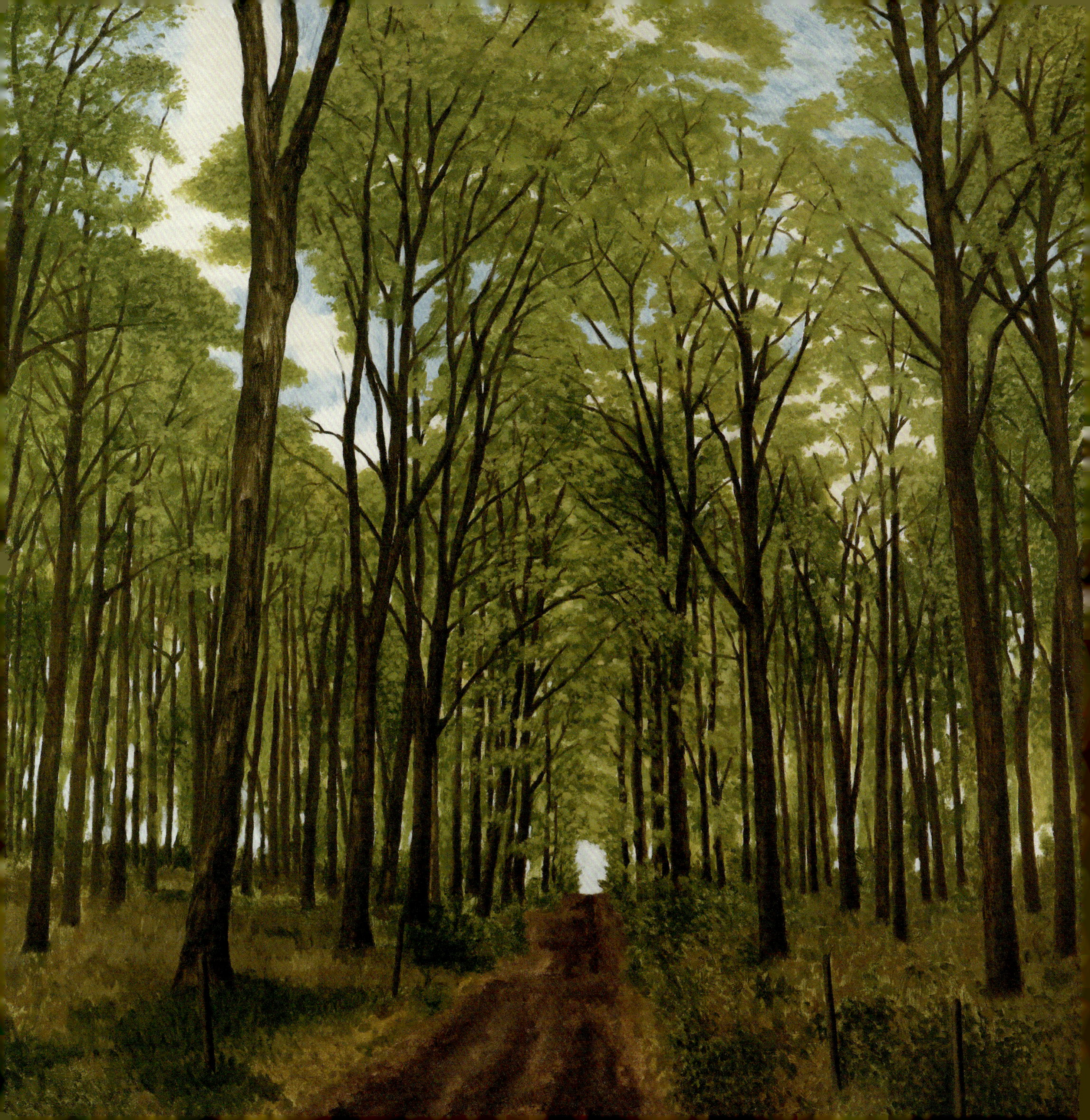

Of All the Luck

Lucky to be an artist at such times
is what you said and I'd agree
believing in the textures, tones;
would glance about us at unfinished,
or framed pictures up on easels.
Some leant against your studio walls.
Despite the lost materials
they're not making any more,
close-weave canvases with feeling
of resistance, but receptive,
David, you can still assemble
shapes such as those shadowy boughs
stenciled on a lit, white gable,
part of the endless-visible
made tender, warmer than before.

Lucky to be an artist at such times
and what you might have meant
was luck in having got this far,
a gamble on not much at the start –
that life class glimpsed, fine teacher,
the risk of harm to self and other …
Yet, still, you'd find in art
not the hymn-sheet sound-bites
repeated like stuck records,
but *Incident off the Dorset Coast*
with lifeboat, ship on fire, a raptor
striking in that *Wiltshire Landscape*,
a red flag, *Hercules*, helicopter …
and see the feeling of these scenes
was yours and yours alone.

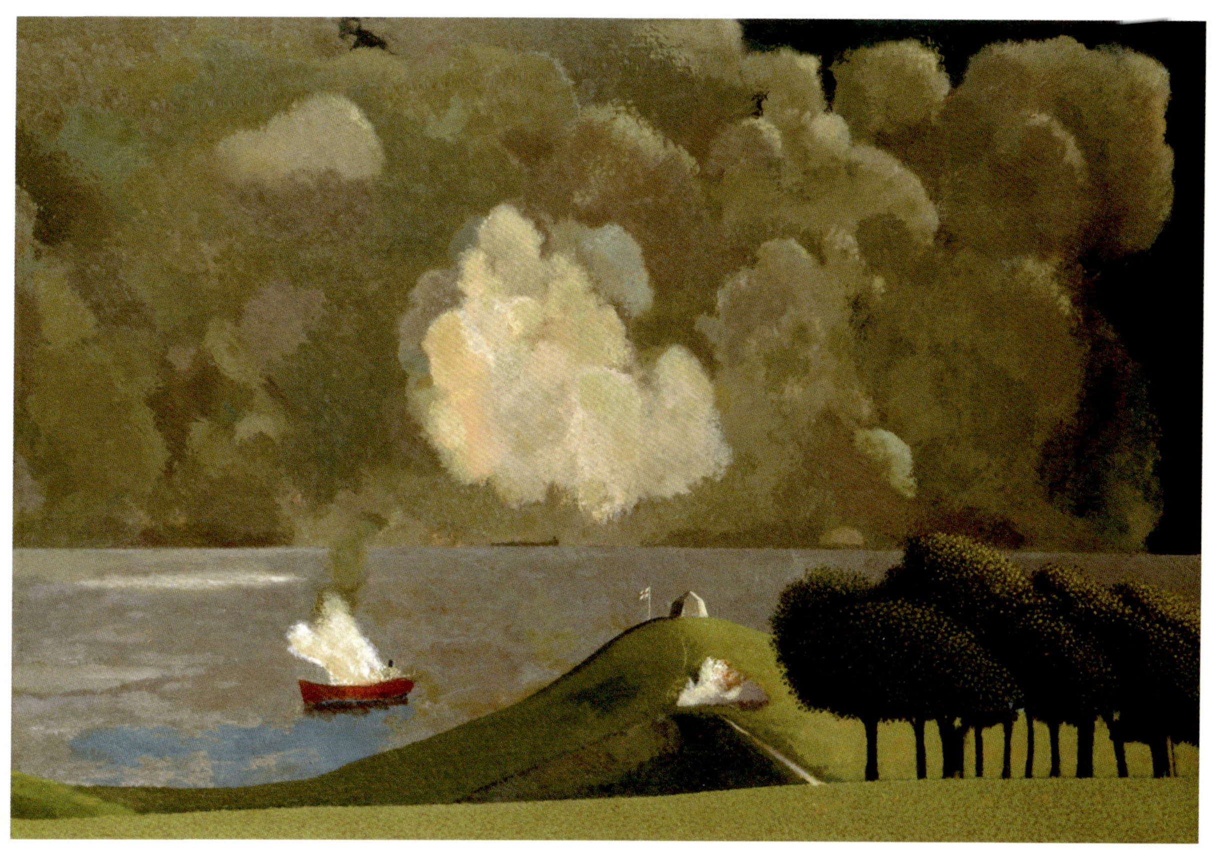

Incident off the Dorset Coast (1984)
Oil on canvas, 58×81cm

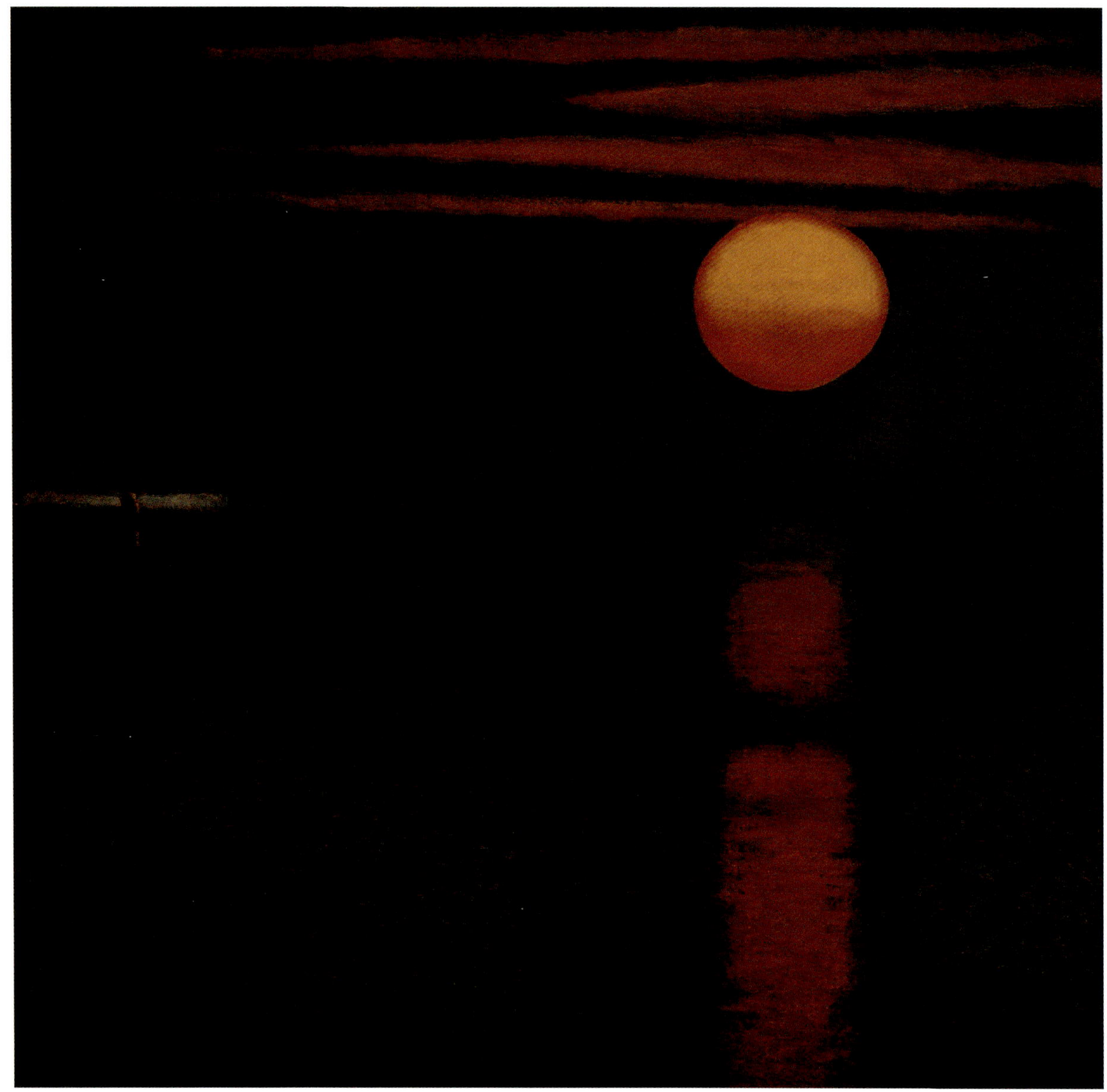

Inshore Waters

1. SEAVIEW TERRACE

Stood still on a high sash-window sill
one rainy day to watch the ships,
staring, still, from that fourth-floor window
I'd see the pin-striped-funnel-line
ferries for Norway disappear,
as if a buried memory
from whence it was we might have come –
another possibility
gone beyond wave-dashed embraces
of its North and South Pier.

2. THE VERY WORDS

Through a July heat wave, now, rain tones
are no more than a memory,
their pain thresholds quite out of view;
a stray shriek, solitary seagull's
in the hazed blue sky
and far from any coast as it's possible to be,
starts up in me, when, down below,
un-worded by a different blue
all I can do is re-echo its cry.

3. COAST PATH

As a Gustave Courbet at Palavas or Trouville,
we're both of us like that Japanese
poet I translated, her need to have the sea's
presence near, its up-reflected light
set off by calm horizons –

Sunset, West Bay (2011)
Oil on canvas, 24×24 inches

or a sign-post for one National Trust
Coast Path, a gannet, or raven's 'Nevermore!'
with banded sunset's acid yellow
shafts on West Bay tides
and an artist under chalk cliffs by that shore.

Coast Path, Dorset (2012)
Oil on canvas, 24×24 inches

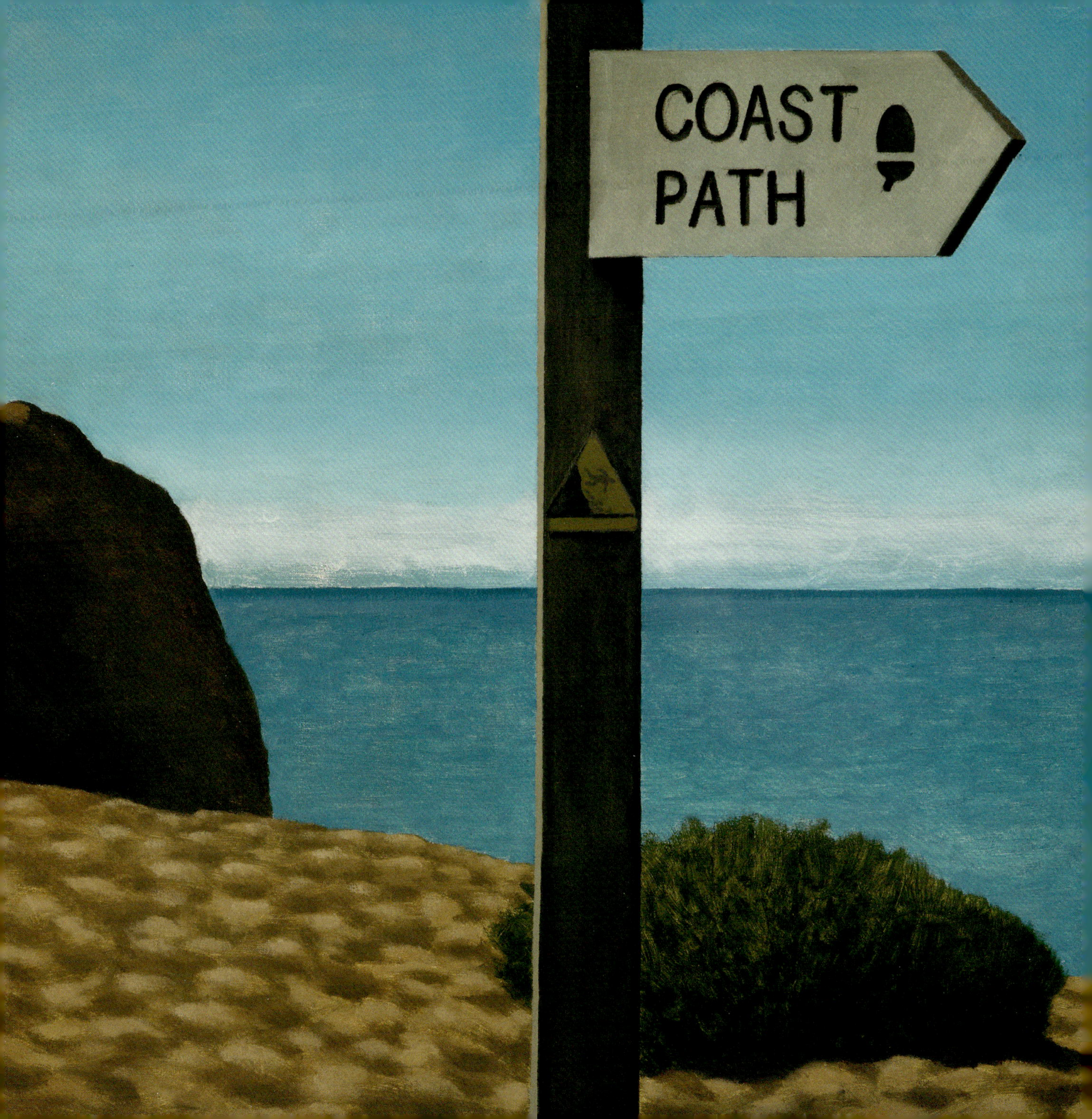

COAST
PATH

At Slader's Yard

There's a corrugated-iron roof,
its undulations flattened
by settled years of lime-green moss;

it juts into repurposed space
where stone-wall textures are revealed,
enhanced by sparser finishes,
framed pictures hung against it:

a dusk cloud risen behind its hill,
the portrait of one tree in moonlight,
another strafing seagull …

They emphasize the edges
letting on bare sail-loft opposite:
a dried grey wood interior
where all the thrifty meanings start.

Then, me too, I'm a counter of clouds
come over the hills like this one
'salmoning' in a 'deepening blue';

they fill up turning windscreen glass
(you see I've put the car in too)
above West Bay's horizon

with a borrowed sharpness, focus
from promptings given by
that pink house under its precipitous cliff.

Recounting them, you're at least alive to
how this word-cloud builds and disperses
ideas like a Nordau's or Lombroso's –

and how they're clouds themselves, these verses.

Tree and Moon (2012)
Oil on canvas, 91.5×91.5cm

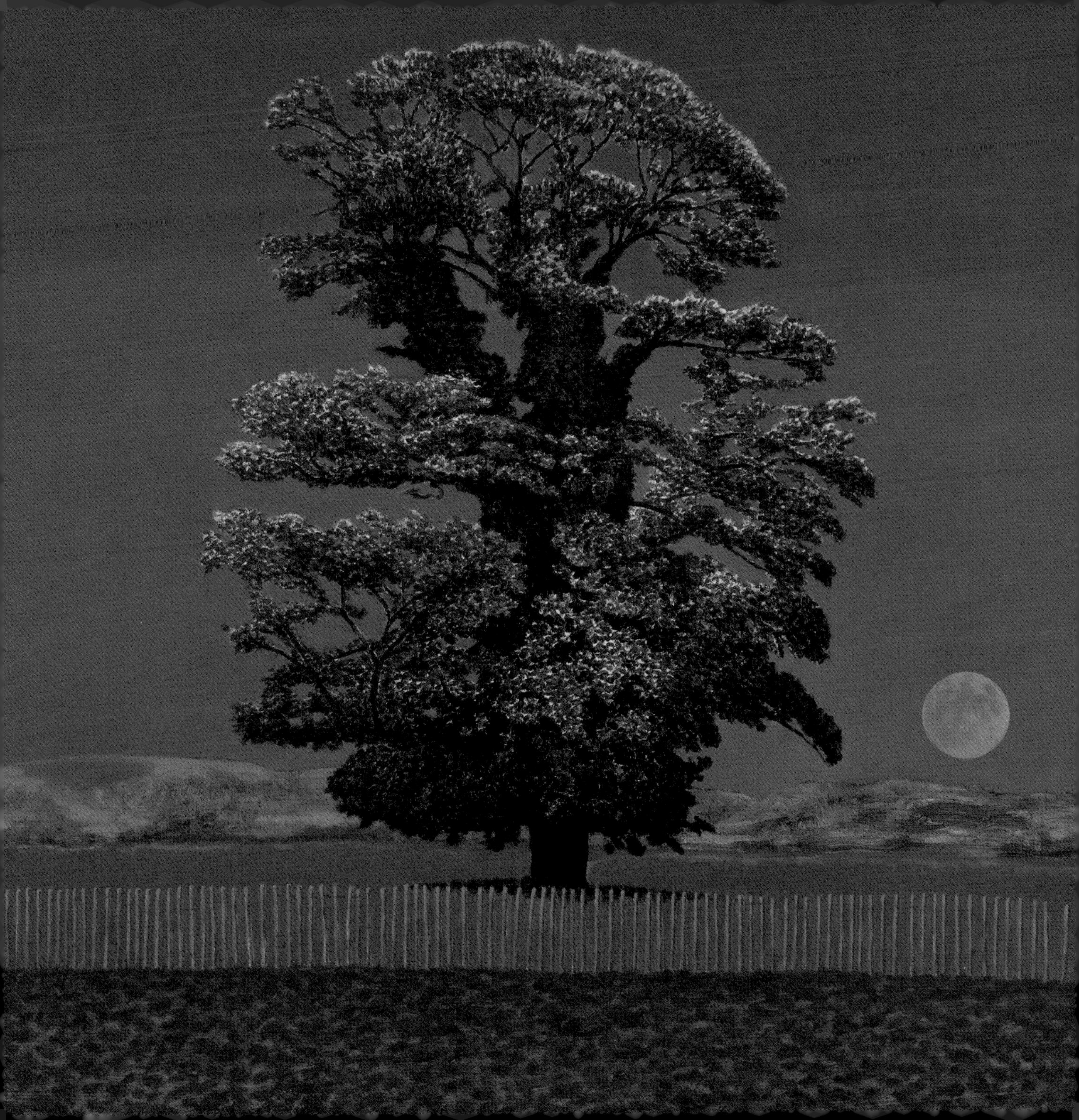

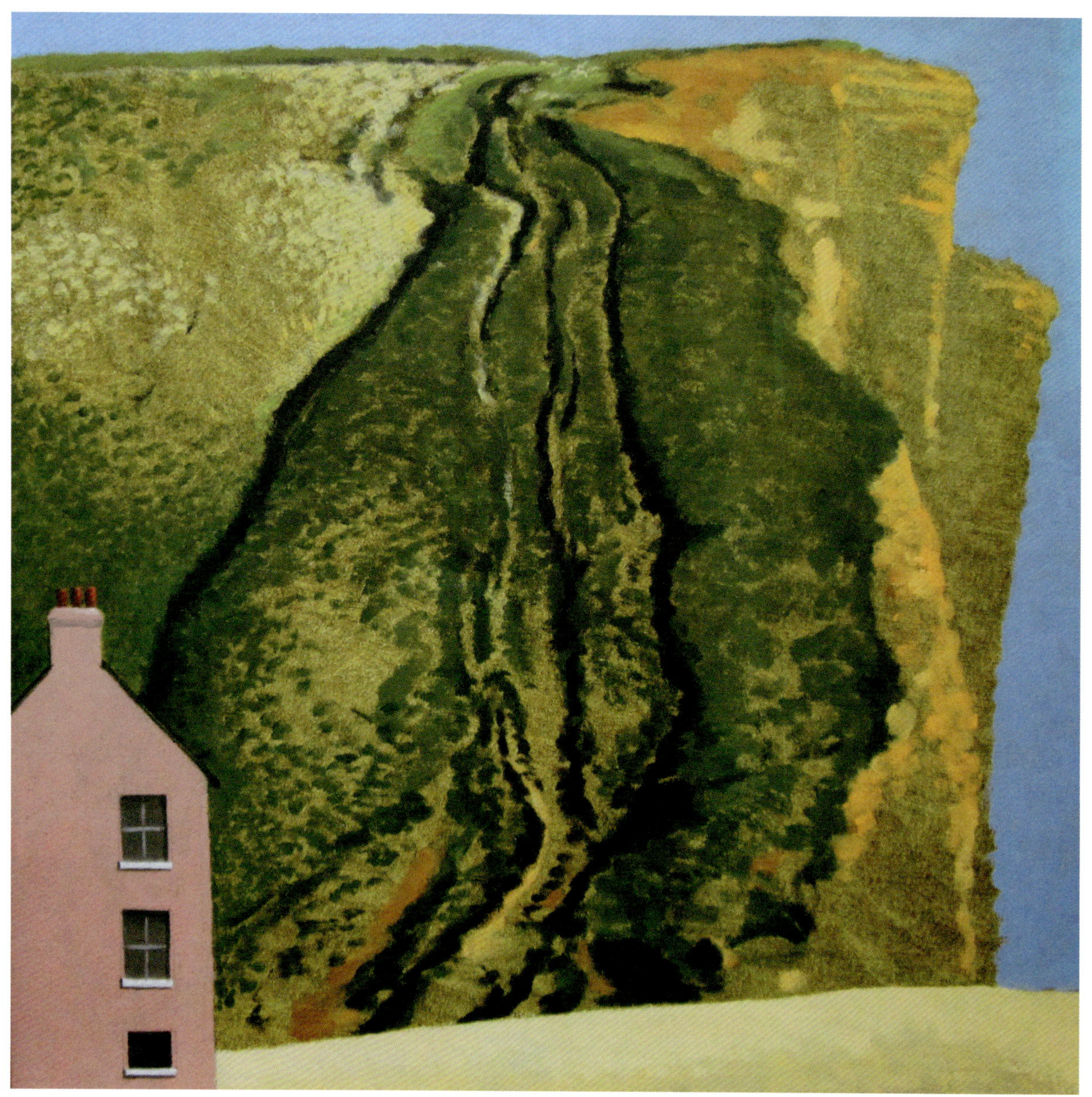

East Cliff, West Bay

'like a dilapidated concertina …'
Simon Rae on West Bay's cliffs

I was searching out your likely viewpoint
where a puce house in the foreground
might line up with cliffs behind

fish-dock scents from floats and nets,
lobster pots, gear, rusted tackle,
painted seagulls' cries!

*

Friable, fissured, the yellow sandstone
cliff with that precarious lean
and terrifying rain erosion

is like a disestablished abbey
looming out of ruination,
oppressive in its size.

*

We're paused below a bank of sand,
grey clouds rising, sea defences,
when momently the cover's riven

only a crack by angled sunlight
flickering back their sudden shadows,
those taking exercise.

*

Pink House, East Cliff, West Bay (2014)
Oil on canvas, 24×24 inches

With salt-spray hazes rearing at them,
beachcombers in its shade
find amongst those wave-smoothed pebbles

unnatural speckling brings the tragic
sense of landscape to this scene,
and our sorry eyes.

East Cliff, West Bay (2004)
Oil on canvas, 117×117cm

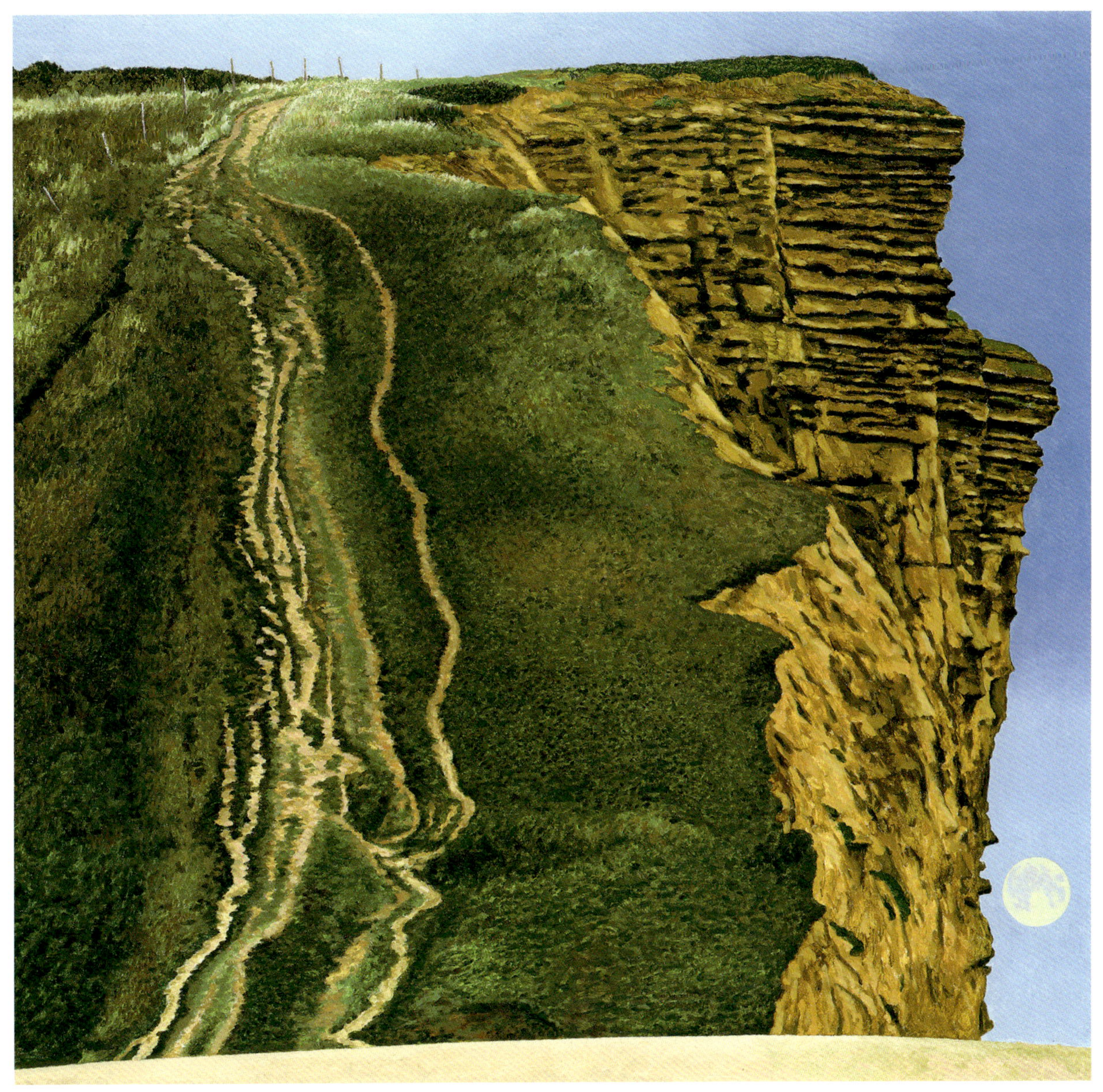

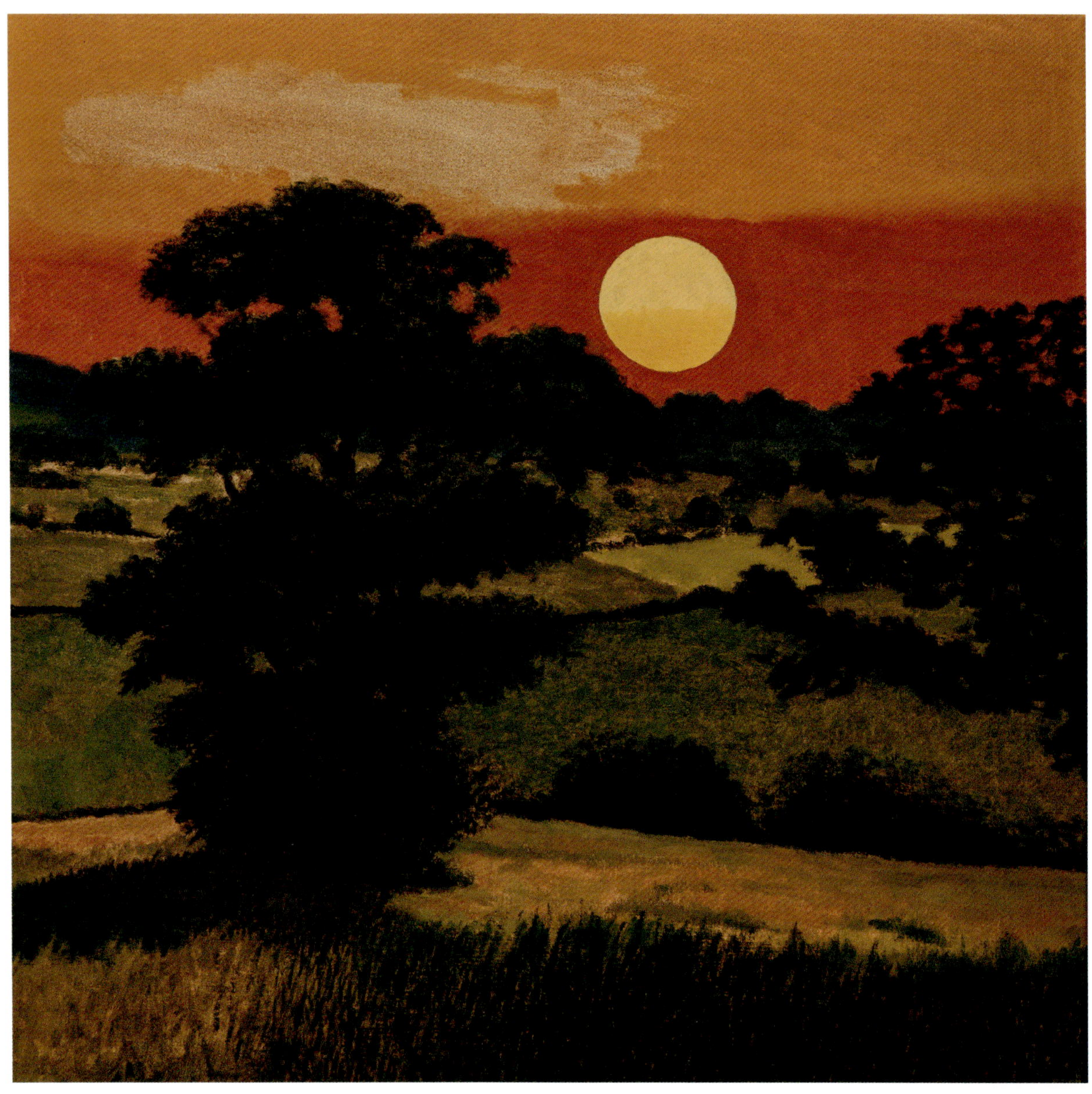

After the Visit

'Voilà un homme qui a découvert
la tragédie du paysage.'
David d'Angers, Dresden 1834

Later, returning, through the turning windscreen
comes what must be Avebury
as we skirt a single standing stone;

and there amongst reminiscent, pinked cirrus
spreads your obligatory grey one –
sensible, a roof-slate-coloured
cloud in unfolding night above us.

We're not alone, still in conversation,
like *Rückenfiguren* at twilight, done
by 'what's-his-name,' as your friend would say,
'that German bloke who paints like you …'

She was home from a Paris retrospective
and, David, in your studio
you'd told us, elated and alive
at such an affinity – elective or no.

Before us while you work on, dusk
shades blind corners we've to drive,
dark edges looming out at us.

Then the starkness of those winter branches'
black against a glowing skyline,
thanks to you, it good as clinches;

it brings back the sense of some design,
and a meaning to this scene.

Sunset, Quantocks (2019)
Oil on canvas, 24×24 inches

Notes

Bonjour Mr Inshaw alludes to *La Rencontre ou Bonjour, Monsieur Courbet* (1854) as well as to T. S. Eliot's 'Little Gidding' and Thomas Hardy's 'The Darkling Thrush'.

Some Recollections is the title of Emma Lavinia Gifford's memoir of her life with Hardy. The shoes have been lent to Strindberg's Miss Julie as a tribute to Cheryl Campbell's performance as the title character in a staging I saw in 1983.

In the Seventies: The epigraph is a refrain line in Hardy's poem whose title I have stolen. The full title of the painting in the second verse is *Lovers near Kew Gardens* (1976).

After Courbet: *L'Origine du monde* was painted in 1866. Attempts have been made to identify whose pudendum it renders, one suggestion being that of Jo Hiffernan, then mistress of James McNeill Whistler.

Mr Manners: '*Tristezza, per favore va via*' [Sadness, please go away] is the opening phrase in Ornella Vanoni's 1967 hit 'Tristezza', an Italian lyric written by Alberto Testa adapting the 1965 Portuguese song 'Tristeza' by Haroldo Lobo and Niltinho. *Il pezzo della vergona* means 'the piece of shame'. The 'virility' interpretation of this custom is from Sicily.

Haunting Landscapes: Figuring in the first stanza are *The Badminton Game* (1972), *Our days were a joy and our paths through flowers* (1972), *The Raven* (1971) and *She Did Not Turn* (1974). Those in the final stanza are *Victoria Dover Calais Paris* (1964) and *My Feeling for a fish a girl and an aeroplane* (1969), destroyed by fire in 2009.

Conversation Piece was prompted by seeing a photograph of *The Meal* in its earlier state with the painted-out hand gesture of the artist holding his chin – from a self-portrait by Degas.

Back Door Moments: David Inshaw's *Juliet* (1980) was painted for the cover of the Arden Shakespeare (second series) edition of the play, first published in that same year. Romeo speaks the epigraph's words in Act 3 Scene 5 of the play.

The Galleries: It was my mother who made the remark that Jackson Pollock's drip paintings look 'like thoughts, mad maps of all our days' at the *Blind Spots* exhibition.

In the High Street: The epigraph is from Bernard Spencer's 'Fluted Armour', where the poet escapes a disintegrating London day by visiting the National Gallery and finds respite in paintings by Pollaiuolo, Bronzino and Piero di Cosimo.

Postcard Concertina: The Thomas Nagel epigraph engages with Bernard Williams' 'moral luck' theme in *Mortal Questions* (1979). These 'postcards' also allude to Carel Fabritius's *The Goldfinch* (1654), Caspar David Friedrich's *Woman at a Window* (1822) and Salvador Dali's *Figure at the Window* (1925).

Remembered Scenes: The epigraph is from 'Wittgenstein and Idealism' in Williams' *Moral Luck* (1973). The paintings recalled in the penultimate scene are Meindert Hobbema's *The Avenue at Middelharnis* (1689) and *The Beech Forest* (1885) by Ferdinand Hodler.

Of All the Luck: The title essay from *Moral Luck* (1973) is alluded to here, an essay in which Williams focuses on the inescapable contingencies in both love and art by exemplifying his arguments with the case of Paul Gauguin risking everything to paint, and Anna Karenina doing the same to be with Vronsky.

At Slader's Yard: The poem is set in and around the gallery and restaurant in West Bay. The quoted phrases are from my early poem called 'Some Hope'. Max Nordau (1849–1923) and Cesare Lombroso (1835–1909) were both social Darwinist believers in inherited criminal characteristics and degeneracy, who thought that there was an identifiable artistic type of 'head in the clouds' character.

Inshore Waters: My maternal grandparents lived at 22 Sea View Terrace, South Shields. The third section also alludes to Courbet's *The Artist on the Seashore at Palavas* (1854) and Whistler's *Courbet at Trouville (Harmony in Blue and Silver)* (1865).

East Cliff, West Bay: The poet Simon Rae's suggestive phrase, adopted as the epigraph, appears in a brief essay he wrote for an exhibition catalogue.

After the Visit: The epigraph ('Here is a man who has discovered the tragedy of the landscape') was reported of the German painter by this French sculptor after a visit to Caspar David Friedrich's studio. *Rückenfiguren* (back-turned figures) can be found in many of his most characteristic landscapes.

Two Rivers Press has been publishing in and about Reading
since 1994. Founded by the artist Peter Hay (1951–2003), the press
continues to delight readers, local and further afield, with its varied list
of individually designed, thought-provoking books.

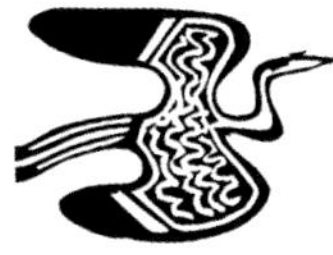